Home Office Research Study 266

Between the lines: an evaluation of the Secured Car Park Award Scheme

David G Smith Mick Gregson and James Morgan

The views expressed in this report are those of the authors, not necessarily those of the Home Office (nor do they reflect Government policy).

Home Office Research, Development and Statistics Directorate
March 2003

Home Office Research Studies

The Home Office Research Studies are reports on research undertaken by or on behalf of the Home Office. They cover the range of subjects for which the Home Secretary has responsibility. Other publications produced by the Research, Development and Statistics Directorate include Findings, Statistical Bulletins and Statistical Papers.

The Research, Development and Statistics Directorate

RDS is part of the Home Office. The Home Office's purpose is to build a safe, just and tolerant society in which the rights and responsibilities of individuals, families and communities are properly balanced and the protection and security of the public are maintained.

RDS is also part of National Statistics (NS). One of the aims of NS is to inform Parliament and the citizen about the state of the nation and provide a window on the work and performance of government, allowing the impact of government policies and actions to be assessed.

Therefore –

Research Development and Statistics Directorate exists to improve policy making, decision taking and practice in support of the Home Office purpose and aims, to provide the public and Parliament with information necessary for informed debate and to publish information for future use.

First published 2003

Application for reproduction should be made to the Communication Development Unit, Room 201, Home Office, 50 Queen Anne's Gate, London SW1H 9AT.

© Crown copyright 2003   ISBN 1 84473 000 X

ISSN 0072 6435

Car parks account for 22% of all vehicle crime and in terms of specific parking locations, cars parked in public car parks are at most risk of theft. The Secured Car Park (SCP) scheme was established by the Association of Chief Police Officers (ACPO) in 1992 to encourage those responsible for car parks to improve security as a means of reducing criminal activity, the fear of crime and the perception of crime in all car parks and vehicle retention areas. This report provides the findings of a national evaluation to determine the effectiveness of the Secured Car Park scheme in reducing vehicle crime.

There are currently just over 1,000 car parks with SCP awards (out of an estimated total of 20,000 car parks). The number of car parks in the scheme has grown at a steady rate since the scheme was revised in 1997 though membership is unevenly distributed across the country. While, as a general pattern, those areas with high levels of vehicle crime have relatively more car parks in the scheme, take up has been particularly low in some high-crime urban areas.

The report in the first instance describes the history of the SCP scheme and goes on to describe the distribution and awareness of the scheme. An analysis of levels of crime and fear of crime in car parks is described in detail and the cost effectiveness of the scheme is also examined. The report concludes with proposals to increase the awareness and take up of the scheme and recommendations relating to taking the scheme forward in the future.

The report finds that the scheme can help reduce the level of vehicle crime and fear of crime in car parks and has acted as a driver for car park improvements in some areas. However, the impact of the scheme has been limited by its relatively low take up. It can be difficult to encourage car park operators to improve security in the face of other financial imperatives; however, the scheme is one of the few levers at the disposal of the police to encourage security improvements to be made.

The report recommends that the organisation and structure of the scheme should be reviewed and a strategic plan be developed outlining how the take the scheme forward and that public awareness of the scheme is increased to help stimulate demand for the scheme.

Carole F Willis
Head of Policing and Reducing Crime Unit

Acknowledgements

The authors would like to thank the many car park operators, police representatives and others for their assistance and patience during the course of this evaluation. Our thanks also go to members of Vehicle Crime Reduction Action Team (VCRAT) and the scheme's administrators for their co-operation and support. Ian Betts is kindly thanked for supplying personal papers covering the history of the development of the award scheme. We would also like to thank Brian Hewitt for conducting the security surveys. Many thanks also to Ruth Goodfield, Tony Holden and Antoinette Hardy (Holden McAllister Partnership) for their assistance with preparing the report. Finally, we would like to express our gratitude for the excellent support and encouragement provided by Joanna Sallybanks of the Home Office.

The authors

David G Smith is Director of Research and Development at the Holden McAllister Partnership, Nottingham. Mick Gregson is seconded to the Holden McAllister Partnership by the Nottingham Trent University, where he is a Principal Lecturer in Psychology.

James Morgan is a partner in Morgan Harris Burrows.

Contents

Boxes

Figures

Tables

Executive summary

The Secured Car Park (SCP) Award Scheme was established by the Association of Chief Police Officers (ACPO) in September 1992 as an off-shoot of their Secured by Design initiative. The scheme was designed to encourage those responsible for car parks to improve security as a means of reducing criminal activity, the fear of crime and the perception of crime in all car parks and vehicle retention areas. This report describes the findings of an evaluation of the scheme by Morgan Harris Burrows and the Holden McAllister Partnership[1].

Methodology

Six study areas were selected for detailed analysis: Manchester, Nottingham, Cheltenham, Northampton, Canterbury and Daventry. Additional information was also collected from other selected car parks from outside these areas. The study areas were selected to provide variation in terms of several factors, including types of town, vehicle crime rates, types of car park, car park design, and levels of SCP scheme membership. The research consisted of a number of elements: interviews with national representatives of the scheme and other stakeholders; workshops and survey conducted with Architectural Liaison Officers; interviews with local car park operators, police and others; a survey of parkers in the study areas; analysis of crime, disorder and car park usage data; independent security reviews of the selected car parks. A study of the costs and benefits of the Secured Car Park Award Scheme in two study areas was also carried out.

Key findings

Take - up of the scheme

There are currently just over 1,000 car parks in England and Wales with awards (out of an estimated total of 20,000). The number of car parks in the scheme has grown at a steady rate since the scheme was revised in November 1997, though membership is unevenly distributed across the country. While, as a general pattern, those areas with high numbers of vehicle crime have relatively more car parks in the scheme, take-up has been particularly low in some high-crime urban areas. Public awareness of the scheme was found to be low (less than one in five car users in a survey of users had heard of the scheme).

---

1. Changes in the funding and management of the scheme occurred at the end of 2001. Plans are under way to improve aspects of the scheme, for example, a marketing strategy and an SCP website are being developed. This report concentrates on the scheme as it existed up to the end of 2001.

Impact of the scheme

There is evidence that the scheme helps to reduce the level of vehicle crime and fear of crime in car parks when targeted at high-crime car parks and leads to low crime levels in new car parks that are built to achieve the award. New car parks built to award standard also tend to be highly rated by users. Spin-offs of the award scheme include increased partnership working between the police and car park operators and a greater emphasis on car park security in some areas. Similar close working was, however, also seen in other areas where the award scheme has not been adopted. The study shows that although crime levels in car parks can be substantial, a greater volume of crime often occurs against cars parked on the street. Thefts from vehicles in car parks are much more common than thefts of vehicles.

Car park design

Formal surveillance (including patrols), lighting, access control and a good physical appearance of the car park can lead to reductions in car crime (or maintain low crime levels in newly built car parks). These features are also those shown by our survey to be important in helping to reduce the fear of crime. The survey showed that cleaner, lighter and better laid-out parking sites are seen as safer by the public, in terms of both security and personal safety. Those parked in such car parks were less worried about parking than those parked in other locations. Environmental considerations were also shown to be related to levels of concern about being a victim of crime, though this concern was more closely related to general concerns about being victimised, previous experience of victimisation, gender (women were more concerned) and the overall crime rate of the area. However, those with greater concerns about being victimised placed more stress on both personal safety and car security as factors influencing their choice of where to park.

The car parks that were most highly rated in terms of perceived safety and environmental factors (lighting, layout and cleanliness) in the survey were all relatively new multi-storey car parks and all had low levels of vehicle crime. Three out of four of these car parks were SCP car parks. These car parks tend to have both CCTV coverage and staff present on site. In addition, the car parks tend to be well maintained, be clean and light and incorporate other features such as good manoeuvrability in and out of spaces, marked pedestrian walkways, etc. Some of these are not criteria for obtaining an SCP award but do appear to have an impact on reducing fear of crime and on perhaps reducing crime levels.

The car parks in the survey which were viewed least favourably by users were all old surface car parks. Crime levels in these car parks were usually higher than in better ranked surface car parks. They tend to be lacking in formal surveillance and have poorly defined perimeters. It is not possible to say that one type of car park has less crime than others: our results show that there are both high and low crime surface and multi-storey car parks (although the very lowest levels of crime were seen in multi-storey car parks).

It is generally recognised that it is easier to build-in security from the outset rather than modify car parks at a later stage. In some cases, the scheme's guidance manual has been used by car park developers in new developments thereby ensuring that good design features are built-in from the start. Evidence from the research suggests that intrinsic design flaws can be overcome to some extent. It is also recognised that it is generally easier, and less expensive to upgrade surface car parks than old multi-storey car parks, which may have implications for the spread of the scheme.

In line with criteria of the scheme, the management of car parks appears to be a critical factor in developing safer car parks. Those car parks that rank highly in terms of public ratings, crime levels and the views of the independent security adviser tend to be particularly well managed and place a strong emphasis on customer satisfaction. They also generally have a greater level of financial investment and place a greater emphasis on issues such as staff training. Management practices play an important role in the effectiveness of security systems. The research provides evidence that good security can be undermined by poor management practices.

Implementation of the scheme

The standard of security in SCPs varies considerably across the country. This is to be expected to some degree, given the risk-commensurate nature of the award scheme. Some of the levels of security seen in low-crime areas would not be acceptable in higher-crime areas. This can make it easier (and less expensive) for car parks in lower-crime areas to obtain the award, which could have implications for the broadening of the scheme. Some of the variation in standards, however, appears to be due to the inconsistent application of the scheme's criteria. However, whilst security standards did vary, awards tend to be given to car parks that delivered low crime levels.

The impact that the scheme's self-assessment guidance manual has had on improving general standards of security in car parks is difficult to measure. It appears however that, even in those cases where car park operators have decided not to apply for an award, the manual has often been used as a source of reference and ideas. The manual was also rated highly by ALOs attending their 2001 annual conference and the measures advocated in the manual relate closely to the factors shown to affect levels of crime and fear of crime in car parks.

Cost-effectiveness of the scheme

The cost of upgrading a car park (or building a new one) can be considerable and the level of investment required can be a barrier to an operator adopting the scheme. Expenditure is also required to repair, clean and maintain car parks to keep them at a high standard (such regular expenditure is a feature of the better car parks in the study). There is, however, evidence to suggest that improvements to car parks can lead to both increased usage and profits for operators. Increased car park usage can also lead to increased usage of other related services or facilities, which can bring additional benefits for operators, such as increased revenue from rental charges in a shopping centre. Others though, have suggested that the relatively low public awareness of the scheme reduces the commercial advantages of displaying the SCP signage.

In some areas, the award process has acted as an effective driver to improving car park security. One local authority described the benefits of obtaining the award to encourage visitors to the town. Car park security in some areas has, however, improved without direct influence of the award scheme.

Conclusions and way forward

The impact of the scheme has been limited by its relatively low take-up. Furthermore, the common practice of targeting scheme membership towards low-crime car parks that require little improvement has meant that vehicle crime is not reduced in many cases as a result of the award process. This importance of the award scheme in reducing crime is likely to increase if both the number of award scheme car parks and public awareness of the scheme increase (the two are likely to go hand-in-hand). Increased public awareness of the scheme may mean that motorists begin to look for SCPs when choosing somewhere to park, which would possibly stimulate other car park operators to upgrade their car parks. However, the survey showed that proximity to destination is the most important factor that controls choice of parking location and there can be difficulties in trying to persuade owners of well-used car parks to upgrade their levels of security.

Our discussions have shown that support for the scheme is very mixed, with some strong advocates and others that are critical of the scheme. It can be difficult to encourage car park operators to improve security in the face of other financial imperatives and it has been suggested that the award scheme is one of the few levers at the disposal of the police to encourage security improvements to be made. While the SCP scheme is not the only way to improve the security of car parks (and car park security has improved in some locations where the scheme has not been adopted), we would conclude that the award scheme has helped to reduce both crime and fear of crime and has acted as the driver for car park improvements in some areas.

The main conclusions from the evaluation are:

- SCP can help reduce levels of vehicle crime and fear of crime *when targeted at high-crime car parks;*

- the key measures that impact on both crime levels and fear of crime appear to be formal surveillance (including patrols), lighting, access control and the physical appearance of the car park;

- car park management also appears to be a critical factor in running a safe, secure car park;

- new car parks built to SCP standard generally have low crime levels and are highly rated by users;

- car parks with lowest user ratings were all old surface car parks;

  - crime levels in these car parks were generally higher than in better ranked surface car parks;

  - they tend to be lacking in formal surveillance and have poorly defined perimeters;

- improving the security of car parks can lead to increased usage and profits;

- there is some evidence that there is some inconsistent application of the scheme across the country;

- take-up of the scheme has been slow in some areas and public awareness of the scheme is relatively low; and

- the importance of the award scheme in reducing crime is likely to increase if both the number of award scheme car parks and public awareness of the scheme increase.

Background

England and Wales, in comparison with other European countries, suffer from high levels of vehicle crime. This is shown by both police-recorded crime data (Hardy 1998; Barclay *et al.* 2001) and victimisation surveys (e.g. Mayhew and White, 1997). Although vehicle crime levels fell fairly sharply during the 1990s, vehicle crime still remains a problem (Sallybanks and Brown, 1999).

To achieve the Government's target to reduce vehicle crime by 30 per cent over five years the Home Office established a multi-agency group, the Vehicle Crime Reduction Action Team (VCRAT), to co-ordinate efforts to achieve this reduction. One of the first tasks of VCRAT was to commission a review of vehicle crime research and statistics, which noted that, in terms of specific parking locations, those parked in public car parks are at most risk (Sallybanks and Brown, 1999). The report identified some evidence that the Secured Car Park (SCP) Award Scheme can contribute to reductions in vehicle crime (Webster and Pengelly, 1997) and, therefore, recommended that owners of car parks should be persuaded to achieve SCP award status (Sallybanks and Brown, 1999).

The award scheme was established in 1992 by the Association of Chief Police Officers (ACPO) to help combat the rising levels of vehicle crime. Vehicle crime levels had risen sharply at the end of the 1980s, reaching a peak in 1992 of approximately 1.5 million recorded offences of theft of and from vehicles (for this reason, 1992 was declared 'Car Crime Prevention Year'). The scheme was one of a number of measures to counter the problem of car crime. A Joint Steering Group (JSG), with representatives from ACPO and other agencies was formed to oversee the running of the scheme. Following the formation of VCRAT, this group was given responsibility of co-ordinating VCRAT's efforts to reduce crime in car parks.

As Sallybanks and Brown (1999) indicated, there is some evidence that the award scheme has led to reductions in crime but it has never been evaluated at a national level. The Home Office, therefore, contracted Morgan Harris Burrows and the Holden McAllister Partnership to conduct an evaluation of the scheme. This report describes the findings of their evaluation.

Car parks

Car parks come in a range of shapes and sizes, are found in many different locations and settings, serve different functions and are operated by a range of different agencies and organisations. It is estimated that there are approximately 8,500 local authority-owned car parks in England and Wales. A survey of 128 local authorities and 211 NHS Trusts showed that, on average, each local authority contacted controlled 28 car parks, whilst NHS Trust contacts controlled on average 20 car parks (WCJ, 1999a; WCJ 1999b). This figure rises to around 14-15,000 if private sector car parks are also included (Ian Betts, personal communication). These figures do not, however, represent all car parks, in that they exclude car parks attached to public houses, leisure centres, entertainment complexes, hospitals, etc. No figures are available on the numbers of these types of car parks, but one estimate suggests that inclusion of these car parks could increase the total figure for the number of car parks in England and Wales to around 20,000 (Webster and Pengelly, 1997). Establishing a figure for the total number of car parks in the country is hampered by the lack of a clear definition of what constitutes a car park.

Car park designs include multi-storey car parks, surface car parks and underground car parks. Each of these design types is covered by the SCP Award Scheme. A distinction can also be made between car parks whose primary function is to provide a parking service (e.g. a car park serving a town centre) and those where providing parking is a secondary function in support of another service or activity (e.g. an office, pub or leisure centre car park). Both types of car parks are covered by the scheme, as are different types of operators (public and private). Car parks generally provide off-street parking and, as such, roadside bays are generally not counted as car parks (although this distinction is not always clear).

Car parks may be permanent or temporary in nature. Temporary car parks include redevelopment sites, which may be used for parking for a number of years, and also sites that are reserved for parking for set periods of time (e.g. seasonal car parks, car parks operating within set time periods, 'fly car parks'). For example, a grassed area alongside the River Trent in Nottingham is used as a car park for Nottingham Forest Football Club on match days and as a riverside footpath for the rest of the time. Whereas some seasonal car parks and long-term temporary car parks may apply for the SCP award, temporary car parks of the type described are unlikely to apply or qualify for the award.

Off-street parking provision forms an important part of local transport strategies. Each local authority is required to develop a five-year local transport plan (LTP), which is in part a bidding document for central government funds for transport, but is also a strategic planning document which places an emphasis on integrated transport. Guidance on the production of local transport plans (DETR, 2000) notes that *"local authorities need to develop an integrated strategy on parking"* and that *"parking is likely to be a key element in managing demand for car use"*. Local authority parking provision may be inspected as part of the best value process (Local Government Act, 1999). Parking provision may form part of local community plans or strategies. Issues of crime and disorder within car parks may also feature within local crime and disorder reduction strategies.

SCP scheme

The Secured Car Park (SCP) award scheme was established by the Association of Chief Police Officers (ACPO) in September 1992, as an off-shoot of their Secured by Design initiative. The scheme was pioneered by Thames Valley police force and developed in partnership with Derbyshire Constabulary and other forces (Smyth, 1993). It was designed to encourage those responsible for car parks to improve security as a means of reducing criminal activity, the fear of crime and the perception of crime in all car parks and vehicle retention areas.

At its launch, the scheme was described by the then Home Office Minister Michael Jack as, *"a practical way to attack the source of nearly one fifth of car crime"* (quoted in Smyth, 1993). This would be achieved through, *"improved design, better lighting and visible supervision"*. The importance of improving car park safety was reiterated by current Home Office Minister John Denham in 2002: *"safer car parks can play an important role in reducing crime. But some car parks have a bad image. Too many are dingy, poorly lit and potentially unsafe, especially for women and the elderly"* (quoted on 10 Downing Street website).

The scheme was originally administered by the Automobile Association (AA), which also had responsibility for marketing and promoting the scheme, with local inspections being carried out by police Architectural Liaison Officers (ALOs). Guidance was produced on the incorporation of design features to help prevent crime within car parks. The criteria developed for assessment of car parks under the original scheme are described in Box 1. These criteria were most easily met by newly constructed car parks ('new builds'), which could incorporate the design features at the planning stage, or by car parks undergoing major refurbishments (Webster and Pengelly, 1997).

Box 1.1: *The original scheme*

Points were awarded by local police officers as shown below, with different criteria being used for multi-storey and surface car parks. Car parks achieving over 85 points received a Gold Award and those achieving 75 points were granted a Silver Award. Awards lasted for two years, after which the car park had to be re-submitted for inspection.

Multi-storey car parks	Surface car parks
Lighting (25 points)	Lighting (20 points)
Vehicle Entry/Exit (6 points)	Natural surveillance and defined perimeters (20 points)
Parking areas (10 points)	Vehicular access and parking area (14 points)
Largely concerned with ensuring good visibility	
Pedestrian routes (12 points)	*Aims to make sure that only those vehicles that should enter the car park do so, that the layout of the parking spaces and circulation areas maximises visibility, is adequately signed and has speed reduction devices*
Aims to make sure that all those visiting the car park can be seen and reduce opportunity for car park users to fall victim to robbery	
Lifts and stairwells (20 points)	Pedestrian routes (8 points)
Security (20 points)	*All pedestrian entrances should have good surveillance and not allow access by vehicles*
Use of CCTV, manpower, cash security and access	
6 bonus points to be awarded at inspecting officer's discretion	Security (21 points)
	Use of CCTV, manpower, cash security and access
	7 bonus points to be awarded at inspecting officer's discretion

A number of problems were identified with the initial design of the scheme. It was recognised that the poor original design of many car parks prevented them from obtaining the SCP award but that through suitable management practices these deficiencies could be overcome. Difficulties were also recognised in the implementation of the points system and with the two-tier award system, with the silver award being perceived as a "second rate" award by operators.

Recognition of these problems led to a re-design and re-launch of the award in 1997. Under the new scheme:

- the Association of British Insurers (ABI) provided funding to support the scheme;

- representatives from ACPO, the AA, the Home Office, British Parking Association (BPA) and Association of British Insurers (ABI) formed a Joint Steering Group (JSG) to oversee the scheme;

- the award incorporated both design and management features, with car parks assessed under nine headings: surveillance, boundary treatment, lighting, vehicular access, parking area, pedestrian access, security, signage and management practice (Box 2);

- awards last for one year after which the car park operator must apply for re-inspection;

- five Regional Development Managers (RDMs), also referred to as surveyors, were appointed to promote the scheme and to ensure consistency across the scheme. Each RDM covered a large area based upon groupings of police force areas. The RDM who covered North West England also had responsibility for Northern Ireland and a separate RDM covered Scotland (reporting directly to ACPOS[2]). They came from a variety of backgrounds, some were ex-police officers and others came from the commercial sector; and

- the decision for granting an award rests with the surveying officers who are permitted to vary the security criteria or consider alternative features dependent upon local factors (a risk-commensurate approach).

A national target of achieving 2000 award-bearing car parks in England and Wales by the year 2000 was set by the JSG. Each police force was given a target to achieve based pro-rata on the population of the police force areas.

---

2.   Association of Chief Police Officers in Scotland.

Box 1.2:   Award scheme criteria 1997-2002 (reproduced from award scheme manual)

Car parks are inspected on an annual basis at a cost of £150 per inspection (it is possible to negotiate a reduction if several of the operator's car parks are assessed on the same day).

Secured Car Park Self Assessment Questionnaire

Address all sections. Are these features achievable or incorporated into your car park? Only answer YES if you can support it with physical or objective evidence. If the answer is NO then complete the attached Table A (see manual), and identify any other compensatory features incorporated.

Referring to the guidance answer Yes or No

1 Surveillance
   a Surveillance of the site
   b Landscaping of car park

2 Boundary treatment
   a Perimeter treatment
   b Clearly defined site perimeter and designated routes

3 Lighting
   a All lighting to British Standard 5489 Part 9
   b Lighting system to incorporate anti-vandal properties
   c Landscaping does not restrict the effect of the lighting scheme
   d Lighting columns do not aid access over perimeter fencing/walls
   e All services/wiring are enclosed to prevent damage/attack
   f Light coloured surface finishes (enclosed car parks)

4 Vehicular access
   a Narrowed entrance
   b Access and egress points reduced to a minimum and controlled
   c Lockable entrances/exits

5 Parking area
   a Parking in straight rows
   b "One way" circulatory movement with speed reduction facilities
   c "Long stay" areas not identifiable, unless additional security provided
   d Payment meters provided with natural surveillance, illuminated, and regularly emptied
   e Adequate provision for disabled parking
   f Multi-storey car parks
         Structure should not restrict surveillance

Restrict access via half levels
Ramped area provided with rough surfaces
Grilles to openings
g Anti-graffiti materials/surfaces to car park

6 Pedestrian access
a Entrance/exit points reduced to a minimum and controlled
b Entrances/exits to have good natural surveillance
c Internal/external approach routes to have good natural surveillance
d Multi-storey car parks:
Spacious lifts
Surveillance of lift interiors, stairwells and landing areas
Lifts, landing areas and stairs easily accessible to parking levels
Wide stairways and open balustrades
Access doors to allow for surveillance
Stairwells and landing external openings to allow for surveillance
e Lockable entrances/exits

7 Security
a Car park surveillance and security staff
b Secure staff facilities

8 Signage
a Customer Charter clearly exhibited in a prominent position
b Management policy clearly exhibited in prominent position
c Parking charges clearly displayed at all entrances
d Clear signage indicating location of all entrances, exits, lifts, stairwells, payment meters, contact points and parking levels
e Car park areas easily identifiable to record incidents

9 Management practice
a Regular meetings to review car park management systems
b Designated member of staff to control relevant documentation
c Customer complaints and resulting actions recorded
d Incidents of crime recorded with relevant information
e Staff trained in areas of responsibility
f Contact member of staff
g Health and Safety/legal requirements adhered to
h Regular car park cleaning and graffiti management

Further changes to the scheme took place towards the end of 2001, when the ABI's agreed four-year period of sponsorship came to an end and when the AA withdrew from the scheme. Arrangements were made for funding to be provided on a temporary basis by the Home Office and the BPA took over the role of administering the scheme (the Award Scheme manager transferred from the AA to the BPA as part of the new arrangements). Initially, the Home Office agreed to provide £75,000 to fund the scheme for the last six months of the 2001/2002 financial year and then later announced a further £300,000 in 2002/03 to support the expansion of the scheme. The Scottish Executive provides funding for the scheme in Scotland. At the time of writing, negotiations are taking place to secure future funding of the scheme. There are plans to increase the number of RDMs and to amend the guidance manual. Steps are being taken to move from an annual inspection regime to biennial inspections. A web site for the award scheme (www.securedcarparks.co.uk) and a marketing strategy are also being developed. It is too early for the effect of these changes to be assessed and, therefore, this evaluation concentrates on the scheme as it existed up to the end of 2001.

Methodology

Six study areas were selected for detailed analysis: Manchester, Nottingham, Cheltenham, Northampton, Canterbury and Daventry. Additional information was also collected from other selected car parks from outside these areas. The study areas were selected to provide variation in terms of a number of factors, including types of town (major city centres, market town, etc.), vehicle crime rates, types of car park (the sample, for example included local authority-owned and privately-owned car parks, shopping centre car parks, hospital car parks, park-and-ride car parks, etc.), car park design (surface and multi-storey) and also levels of membership of the SCP award scheme.

The research consisted of a number of elements:

- interviews with national representatives of the scheme and other stakeholders;

- workshops and survey conducted with Architectural Liaison Officers at their annual conference in Blackpool 2001[3];

---

3. Six workshops were held with approximately 100 people over the course of two days. In addition, a questionnaire was distributed to attendees. Sixty people, representing 24 different police forces from across the UK, completed and returned questionnaires.

- detailed examination of the study areas, including:

  ❏ interviews with local car park operators, police and others;

  ❏ a survey of car users. A total of 1,875 interviews were conducted with a sample of users of award-bearing car parks, other car parks and those parking on-street across the study areas[4];

  ❏ collection of crime, disorder and usage data. Information was requested, where applicable, for individual car parks within the study areas, for the beats in which the car parks are located and the encompassing police Basic Command Unit (BCU). Crime data were collected from a larger number of car parks than were included in the user survey;

  ❏ independent security reviews[5]; and

- a study of the costs and benefits of the Secured Car Park Award Scheme in two study areas.

The survey of car users was conducted face-to-face with a sample of users in five areas. Three hundred interviews were conducted in each of Canterbury, Cheltenham and Northampton; 375 interviews were conducted in Manchester and 600 in Nottingham. In each location, an area of the town or city where car users were presented with a number of choices of where to park was selected. The survey was designed to cover a range of different types and design of car parks across the sample. People parking at on-street locations close to car parks were interviewed in four of the five towns. One thousand interviews were conducted in multi-storey car parks, 600 in surface car parks and 275 with on-street parkers. Interviews were conducted between the hours of 7am and 7pm.

One of the major obstacles to the research was obtaining accurate crime information. Several of the police forces had difficulties in obtaining data for car parks from their systems and doubted the accuracy of the data sets they provided. In some cases it took police forces several weeks to produce the data and, in other cases, several months. The fact that a crime occurred on a car park is not always recorded. Crime reports may, for example, indicate that a crime took place on Coid Street but may not indicate whether it occurred on the street or on the car park situated on Coid Street. We were made aware of one situation by the

---

4.   Interviews were conducted face-to-face with the car owners by Social Research Associates Ltd.
5.   These were conducted by a Security Consultant, who previously worked at the Home Office Crime Prevention College. Assessments were carried out using a tool based upon the award scheme's self-assessment guidance.

police where crimes occurring on a particular street were being incorrectly recorded as occurring in the car park named after the street. Difficulties also exist over the naming of car parks, with different names being used for the same car park. For example, one car park serving a retail centre was variously described in terms of the name of the road it was situated on (and the name of the main road that this minor road branched from), the name of the site, or the name of various stores on the site. In one area, many of the names of the car parks that occurred in the police data for the town were not recognisable by the local authority (despite being local authority car parks). Similar problems in obtaining information on crime in car parks were described by Webb et al. (1992).

Even greater difficulties were experienced in our request for information on incidents of disorder in car parks. Incidents of disorder could be one of the main factors governing fear of crime (and controlling the choice of where to park) but the difficulties in providing accurate incidents data prevented an examination of such incidents.

The award scheme requires car park operators to maintain a record of crime and other incidents that occur in their car parks but our research revealed that this is not always insisted upon at a local level. In one area, a local authority operator had been told by the local police and RDM that they would not be required to collect their own incident data. In another area, the local authority does maintain records of incidents (though not in an easily usable format) but this information has never been asked for as part of the inspection process. Given difficulties in obtaining local crime data, this lack of information further compounds the difficulty of identifying crime and disorder problems in car parks and also provides an example of the inconsistent application of the scheme (Section 2.3).

A variety of statistical tests were used in the analysis of the data collected for the study. Three-monthly moving averages were used[6] in the analysis of the crime data to lessen the influence of large fluctuations in individual months within the data sets (smoothing the data). The t Test was used to explore for statistical changes in crime levels in the twelve-months before and after changes were made to the security or operation of the car parks. Levels of significance are generally not shown within the report but the convention of indicating differences where $p \leq 0.05$ as significant and differences where $p \leq 0.01$ as very significant has been followed.

A range of statistical tests were used in the analysis of the survey data; chi-squared was the most commonly used but Pearson correlations, t-tests and analysis of variance were also used as appropriate and these are indicated in the relevant sections. Following the

---

6.   Calculated by taking the average over three-months. The moving average 'moves' because, as the newest period is added, the oldest is dropped. For example, April-May-June is then replaced by May-June-July, and so on.

convention above, many of the differences discussed in relation to the survey could be classed as extremely significant in that p<.001 but we have not made use of this phrase. Unless it is stated otherwise all differences or relationships mentioned in the analysis of the survey data are at least very significant (p<0.01). It should be remembered though that even quite small differences can be statistically significant given large enough numbers.

Format of the report

The remainder of this report is divided into four sections, which describe the:

- distribution and awareness of the scheme;

- crime and fear of crime in car parks;

- costs and benefits; and

- conclusions and way forward.

2.   Distribution and awareness of the scheme

Distribution of the scheme

At the start of 2002, there were 1,010 car parks with the SCP award in England. Figure 2.1 shows the growth of scheme membership since the reorganisation of the scheme. Information on the membership of the scheme is maintained on a database by the scheme's administrators, which consists of 21 fields that describe the location, ownership, design and usage of SCPs (market sector). Unfortunately, the database has not been fully maintained and contains a large number of missing entries. For example, contact names are missing for 28 per cent of award-bearing car parks. The database does not provide any information about the crime prevention measures that are present within the car park.

Figure 2.1:   *Secured Car Park Awards November 1997 to December 2001*

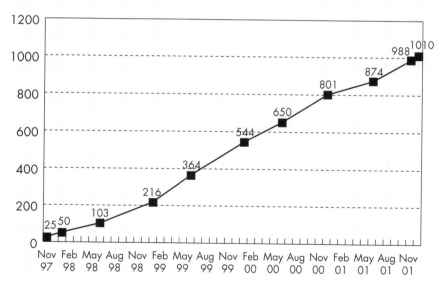

In a third of cases the type of car park is not indicated but of those that are, two-thirds are surface car parks and a third are multi-storey car parks (two are underground car parks, representing less than 1% of the available total). The higher number of surface car parks presumably reflects the greater number of these types of car parks across England and Wales, but may also be a reflection of the greater ease that operators report in upgrading surface car parks to meet the award standard.

The database shows which police force area each car park is situated in (this is the only field with no missing data). Kent Constabulary has the largest number of car parks per force area (112, 12% of all car parks nationally which have the SCP award), whilst there were no award-bearing car parks in areas covered by Dyfed Powys and City of London police forces.

As would be expected, given the variation in size and nature of the areas covered by the various forces, the number of schemes per force area varies considerably. Comparing the number of awards per force area with the number of vehicles crimes in 2000/01 (Povey et al. 2001) shows that as a general pattern, those areas with high numbers of vehicle crime also have the highest levels of awards (and vice-versa). The variation in the number of award car parks per police force area cannot, however, be entirely explained by variations in size, urbanicity or vehicle crime levels of police force areas. For example, Cambridgeshire and Norfolk are amongst the most rural forces (Povey et al. 2001) but there are more award car parks in these force areas than in some of the larger urban force areas. At the start of 2002, there were 40 award car parks in Cambridgeshire and 25 in Norfolk but only six in South Yorkshire, eight in Northumbria and 16 in Merseyside.

Take-up has been particularly low in some of the major cities. For example, there are only nine SCPs in Liverpool and ten in Manchester (two areas with high levels of vehicle crime: Povey et al, 2001). These figures can be compared to smaller areas such as Chatham (21 car parks), Stockton-on-Tees (16) and Swindon (15).

Suggested reasons for the slow take-up of the scheme in some areas

A number of reasons for the slow take-up of the scheme in some areas were suggested in our interviews with local and national representatives. Further suggestions came from a series of workshops with ALOs at their annual conference in 2001 and a questionnaire that was issued to workshop participants. The evaluation did not, however, examine the administration and management of the scheme and the factors listed here are not exhaustive. Furthermore, the factors vary in importance and represent the personal experiences and feelings of those consulted (generally founded on practical experience of the scheme). Some reasons were suggested on several different occasions by a variety of different stakeholders and these are listed below:

Cost of upgrading security and lack of incentives. Car park operators operate in a competitive economic situation and, therefore, persuading them to upgrade security can be difficult. A telephone survey on behalf of the Home Office indicated that the major reason for car parks not being submitted to the scheme was because the level of investment needed was too high (WCJ, 1999a; WCJb). The costs of upgrading the security of car parks can be considerable and some operators have queried whether being a member of the award scheme has any economic advantage (partly linked to the low public awareness of the scheme, see below). This is particularly true where, despite any problems with crime, the car park is being well used (Box 2.1 describes one police force's response to such a problem). Local authorities must work within their budgets and, therefore, have similar financial constraints that may lead them to prioritising other areas than car park improvements for expenditure.

The risk-commensurate nature of the award scheme could make it more difficult to obtain awards for car parks in some high crime areas because of the higher levels of security (and therefore, generally, higher costs) that are required by the surveyors in these areas. This may be one of the reasons for comparatively low take up in some major cities and urban police force areas; although it fails to fully explain the patterns in scheme membership (for example, scheme membership is relatively high in West Midlands police force area compared with other urban areas).

The SCP scheme was contrasted to the Secured by Design award (of which SCP is a sub-branch), where no charge is made to the recipient of the award and, in fact, Housing Associations may actually be financially rewarded for obtaining the award. One ALO commented, "I would like to be able to reward operators for taking steps to reduce crime rather than ask for money [for the inspection] after they had already had a substantial cash outlay".

Box 2.1:   Naming and shaming

An example is provided of where the threat of 'naming and shaming' was used successfully to encourage a reluctant retail park to upgrade the security of its car park, which had persistently high crime rates. Although based upon a real example, the names and locations have been anonymised.

The Hills Retail Park car park has 550 spaces and serves five retail premises and a fast food outlet. The car park has suffered from high crime levels for a number of years and, although crime levels have been falling, improving security in the car park remained a priority for the local community safety partnership. The main offences at the site were thefts from vehicles although there had also been a rape and a case of indecent assault in recent years. The level of crime on Hills Retail Park was more than double the levels at two comparable sites in the same police beat. The police found it useful to use the two comparable sites as an example in discussions with Hills Retail Park, to show what benefits can be achieved from improved security.

A site survey report was produced following an inspection involving the local police, representatives of the local Council's CCTV staff and others. The main problems identified by the inspection were problems with access control, poor maintenance of shrubbery and trees, lack of CCTV coverage and poor lighting. The site was difficult to police with a large number of escape options for offenders. Upgrading the car park to SCP award standard was suggested as an additional (but possibly incremental) consideration.

The police and other agencies recognised that solutions needed to be aimed at the entire retail park and not at individual businesses. For example, it was recognised that customers may park on one part of the car park but use a number of the retail outlets. Therefore improvements would potentially benefit all businesses on the site and there were potential cost savings through a collaborative approach.

The retail park's property agent was encouraged to bid for matched funding from the police for the necessary improvements. Despite being successful in this bid, the agent informed the police that the site's tenants were not willing to pay for the improvements and that the, *"options were not economically feasible for site owners"*. Further negotiations took place and, with most businesses on the site arguing that the responsibility for security improvement lay with the landlord, no agreement could be reached to fund or progress the initiative.

Representatives from the retail park were called to discussion with the local Chief Constable at which the police outlined the problems at the site and some of the potential benefits (such as increased usage). The police acknowledged that the issue of who should pay was a matter to be agreed between the property agent and tenants, but emphasised that the crime levels on the site were unacceptable and improvements to security had to be made. The representatives of the retail park were presented with the option of confirming implementation of security measures and allocation of finances by a set date or the local police force would exercise their duty of care to warn and reassure the public. This would be done by informing the public of the crime problems at the site through the local media, on street lighting columns on the approach to the site and also by promoting the use of the local SCP award car parks on street furniture. The publicity campaign would be planned to coincide with the Christmas and New Year period, so as to *"maximise the potential for crime prevention"*. The representatives were also informed that the police would withdraw their attendance from the site except for certain specific occasions (such as if incidents involved injury to members of the public). It was suggested that this would have clear business and insurance implications because of the lack of police response or allocation of a crime reference number.

This approach was not taken lightly and the police first gained support of all statutory agencies attached to the local community safety partnership, obtained legal advice on their statutory obligations and briefed the local Member of Parliament. The approach achieved the desired results and led to an agreement to upgrade the security without the need for police support being withdrawn. The cost of CCTV and site refurbishments were met by the property agent and tenants and the cost of lighting was met by the land-owner. Matched funding was provided by the police. The police found that this allowed them a greater role in the decision making, since they were viewed as a joint investor rather than just an adviser.

Cost of inspections. Many consultees also thought that the cost of inspections was a deterrent. Some operators claim to be discouraged by the cost of inspections and re-inspection of car parks. Others, however, point out that inspection costs are low compared with the large revenues that can be achieved through charging for parking (although not all award-bearing car parks charge for parking) and that discounted inspection fees can be negotiated where multiple car parks are involved. Further discussion on the costs and benefits of the award scheme is presented in Chapter 4.

Canterbury City Council currently has a large number of award-bearing car parks and, according to the local police and the council, there are a large number of other car parks that could be successfully put forward for the award. The main reason that these car parks have not been put forward is because of the mounting inspection costs and, furthermore, the authority is considering withdrawing from the scheme completely because of annual inspection costs. Canterbury's Parking Services Manager observed that, *"I don't have a budget for membership of award schemes, the inspection costs have to come out of the maintenance budget and the money might be better spent on other things"*. One hospital withdrew its six car parks from the scheme because of the need to make cost savings across the hospital's services and the inspection fees were seen as a non-priority area that could be easily cut. Another local authority questioned whether spending money on inspections represented 'best value'.

Lack of operators' liability for crime in car parks. It has been suggested that the lack of operators' liability for crimes occurring in their car parks has served to lessen the likelihood of an operator improving security, especially where crime problems are not leading to a loss of revenue (e.g. Which?, 1990; RAC, 1991; Webb et al., 1992; Pengelly, 2000; AA, 2002). This is a contentious issue with many operators arguing that this would affect operators' ability to trade profitably. At least one car park operator does, however, currently voluntarily guarantee the safe-keeping of customers' vehicles and will meet the costs involved in any incident of theft of or from vehicles in the car park. Some have pointed to local authorities, obligations under Section 17 of the Crime and Disorder Act (1998), which requires them to *"do all* [they] *reasonably can to prevent, crime and disorder..."*. There is a possibility that local authorities can be challenged by judicial review if it can be shown that they have not taken reasonable steps to prevent crime in their car parks (see, for example, Moss and Pease, 1999 and Moss and Seddon, 2001 for a discussion of crime prevention and planning).

Enthusiasm for scheme and pre-existing state of car parks. It has been suggested that the variation between areas reflects differing levels in enthusiasm that police forces and local operators have for the scheme and the pre-existing state of the car parks in the areas (i.e. ease of upgrade, which in turn is linked to costs). For example, we were made aware that the majority of car parks that are currently within the scheme were put forward because they required little modification to meet the scheme's requirements and already had low crime levels. Clearly this makes it easier to expand the scheme in some areas than others. The number of award-bearing car parks in an area can increase dramatically if large operators (such as the local authority) can be persuaded to upgrade their car parks to achieve the award. The relatively high number of SCP car parks in two of the study areas can mainly be attributed to the local authorities operating the majority of car parks in these areas and both authorities having been very committed to the scheme for some time. Areas with a large number of operators pose more difficulties for RDMs and local police officers in that each individual operator needs to be convinced of the benefits of joining the scheme.

It was suggested during interviews with several stakeholders that the spread of the scheme has been hampered by the failure to gain the support of several key players, including some local authorities and large private car park operators, supermarkets and hotel chains[7]. Figures for the leading private operators show that, for example, across the UK they have 740 off-street contracts, manage 2,303 sites and own 103 others but operate only 139 sites with SCP awards (Parking Review, 2001). Many of these sites are in high-profile city centre locations, which it can be argued could impact on public awareness of the scheme (see below). Criticism was expressed about the lack of discussions at a national level to gain support of these national chains, although we understand that some negotiations have taken place but without success.

---

7.   Hotel car parks, particularly those used by business people, were commonly identified by the police as vehicle crime hotspots.

Relatively low awareness of the scheme. Most of the people we spoke to commented upon the lack of public awareness of the SCP award scheme (which was linked by people to a lack of marketing of the scheme, for example through road signage and publicity) and suggested that this had contributed to the slow adoption of the scheme by operators. Some police officers suggested that take-up of the award scheme would remain low until the public began demanding safer car parks.

A telephone survey commissioned by the Home Office[8] revealed that whilst 96 per cent of local authorities had heard of the award scheme, only 34 per cent of NHS Trust contacts and 53 per cent of the other types of operators (universities, retailers and rail operators) had (WCJ, 1999a; WCJ 1999b). RDMs subsequently targeted action at these areas to raise levels of awareness of the scheme and there are now a number of hospitals on the scheme. Home Office ministers also wrote to all MPs in February 2001 urging them to promote the scheme. A series of regional conferences were also held in October 2000 to raise awareness amongst target groups.

Levels of awareness of the scheme were also examined as part of this evaluation through a survey of car users. Our survey reveals a relatively low public awareness of the scheme, with only 18 per cent of respondents overall being aware of the scheme. More of those respondents parked in SCPs (22%) had heard of the scheme compared with those parked elsewhere (14%). The results, and issues surrounding awareness of the scheme, are discussed further in the following section.

Use of the word 'secured'. The guidance for the scheme makes clear that its objective is to certify car parks which have introduced effective measures to create a safe and secure environment which reduces public fears and restricts opportunities for crime to be committed. Nonetheless, concern was expressed about the name of the award scheme. It was widely felt that the name is misleading to the general public because it implies a higher level of security than is the case[9]. At least one local authority (Canterbury) has decided not to publicise that their car parks are part of the award scheme for fear of misleading the public (and potential embarrassment if crimes occur in car parks that they have advertised as 'secured'). Similar concern was expressed about the new road signage for secured car parks, with one local authority representative of the BPA indicating that he would not use the signage. Concern was also expressed that the use of the word 'secured' could open car

---

8.   There were a total of 367 responses to the telephone survey. The numbers who responded were as follows: Rail operators =8, Universities = 23, NHS Trusts = 207, Retailers =1, Local authorities = 128

9.   Many referred to the dictionary definition of the word secure. For example the Oxford Pocket Dictionary defines secure using terms such as 'untroubled by danger or fear', 'impregnable', 'certain not to fail', 'fortify, and 'guarantee, make safe'.

park operators up to claims of liability if someone was a victim of crime on an SCP[10]. The "Safer Car Park Scheme" was offered as an alternative by some.

Awareness of the Secured Car Park award scheme

A concern commonly expressed by those involved with the award scheme is that it is not well known among the public. The survey supports this concern: overall only 18 per cent of respondents claimed to have heard of the scheme. More of those respondents parked in SCPs (>22%) had heard of the scheme compared with those parked elsewhere (<14%)[11].

Awareness of the scheme varied considerably from place to place. Generally the area differences were in line with what might be expected on the basis of the extent of local publicity; thus, for example, more than 25 per cent of Nottingham respondents, where the scheme has received relatively more publicity, had heard of it compared with less than 10 per cent of those from Manchester (the corresponding figures for the other sites were: 12 per cent in Canterbury; Cheltenham 21 per cent; Northampton 18 per cent). With the exception of Northampton, multi-storey car park users were generally more likely (23%) to be aware of the scheme than those parked in surface car parks or on the street (12.5%)[12]: greatest awareness being claimed by those parked in SCP multi-storey car parks in Nottingham (31%) and least by Manchester street parkers (5%). Only in one car park did the number of respondents aware of the SCP scheme equal the number who was not. This was Talbot Street multi-storey in Nottingham that is noteworthy both for the extent of its signage indicating membership of the scheme and significant local publicity for the car park.

When respondents parked in a car park were asked whether they were parked in a SCP award scheme car park, most (71%) did not know. Sixteen per cent of those parked in an SCP recognised that they were, but eleven per cent of those in non-SCP car parks also thought they were parked in a scheme car park. While this difference is statistically very significant it is not large. Among those who had heard of the scheme nearly half (47%) of

---

10. The scheme manual states that possession of the award does not guarantee a crime- free car park and that it should be made clear that granting an award does not create any liabilities to the owner or operator over and above their general contractual and tortuous obligations. The JSG has indicated that, in line with normal practice, local operators have to obtain their own legal advice on their position in the light of particular circumstances.
11. To remind the reader, all differences presented here deriving from analysis of the survey are very significant unless it is stated otherwise. In fact, this particular difference is extremely significant (p<.001) statistically.
12. In Northampton there was a slight non-significant tendency for street parkers (22%) to be more aware of the scheme than multi-storey (19%) or surface (15%) car park users.

those parked in a SCP correctly said that they were. However, this is not significantly different from the 42 per cent who were not parked in an SCP but who claimed that they were. This suggests that a general awareness of the scheme does not necessarily translate into an awareness of the status of specific car parks.

Again there were marked regional variations. Table 2.1 shows the percentage of car park users who said they were parked in a SCP.

Table 2.1: *Percentage of car park users who thought they were parked in a Secured Park Car Award Scheme car park*

	Car park users who had heard of the SCP award (N=303)		All car park users (N=1572)	
	Secured car parks	Non SCP car parks	Secured car parks	Non SCP car parks
Canterbury	13.0	69.2	2.3	15.0
Cheltenham	41.7	0.0	14.3	1.3
Manchester	60.0	44.4	24.5	13.2
Northampton	31.6	16.7	10.5	6.0
Nottingham	62.2	42.1	27.2	12.1
Overall	46.7	41.8	16.3	11.2

While there is a general failure among SCP users to realise that they were in a SCP, Canterbury is unusual here in that almost no-one (just 2% overall or 13% of those who had heard of the SCP award) parked in an SCP realised that they were and indeed those parked in the one non-SCP car park in the sample were more likely to think that they were in an SCP. This can be understood in terms of the lack of signage or advertising in the area and the fact that the non-SCP car park has not been submitted for the award only because of the cost of doing so rather than because of its characteristics. Signage and publicity seem to be key aspects of awareness. For example, in the Talbot Street car park mentioned above 88 per cent of respondents who had heard of SCP correctly said that it was an award scheme member.

Security and quality of award car parks

The main security criteria that appear to be used for making the award are the presence of CCTV, good lighting and lack of areas for concealment (probably in that order). Crime levels were also taken into consideration when making awards. This finding is supported by the results of a telephone survey conducted on behalf of the Home Office, which showed that of those contacts that were planning to improve their car parks to award scheme standard, the most common steps being taken were to improve lighting and install CCTV (WCJ, 1999a; WCJ 1999b). The large range of other criteria described in the self-assessment guidance is less commonly insisted upon. For example, the presence, or otherwise, of perimeter fencing varies between car parks and the definition of a help point varies between areas. In some cases, for example, a help point consists of only a sign pointing to the nearest public telephone and in others the car park user can speak directly to a control room (and may be monitored by CCTV at the same time). In some cases, operators have been asked to improve features that relate more to car park 'quality' than security (for example, the results of one inspection recommended that directional arrows and bay marking be re-painted). We found, however, that despite the variations in application of the scheme, the award tends to be given to car parks that delivered relatively low crime levels.

The award scheme manual states that the surveying officers may, *"vary the security criteria or consider alternative features dependant (sic) upon local factors"*, thus ensuring a risk-commensurate approach, but the extent to which surveying officers can vary these criteria is not specified. Our research, however, reveals a common belief that the award scheme is being inconsistently applied across the country. The survey of ALOs, for example, revealed that around a third of survey respondents had seen car parks with the SCP award that they did not think meet the required standard. One ALO admitted that the findings of a security survey would differ depending upon which of his colleagues conducted the survey and one RDM spoke of the higher standard that one of his colleagues was able to insist upon in his area. The independent security reviews that were commissioned as part of this evaluation indicated that, based upon the surveyor's examination of the security provision within the car parks, around a third of car parks with the SCP award were lacking in aspects of security[13]. A representative from one countrywide car park operator also observed regional variation in the criteria used for the award: *"you might get the award for a car park in one area that you wouldn't in another"*.

Perceptions of SCP scheme car parks

Are SCPs viewed as having the qualities of safe car parks and as being safer than non-SCPs? Do people parked in SCPs have fewer concerns about parking there than those parked in other car parks or on the street? These are important questions but difficult to

---

13. The surveyor did not take into account local crime rates when making his assessment. The award scheme manual is, however, vague about how much influence local crime rates should have on the decision-making process.

answer because of the implicit phrase *all other things being equal* within each question. Simple comparisons of perceptions of SCPs and non-SCPs are problematic because all other things are not equal. For example, there are area-based differences in the likelihood that a car park will belong to the SCP scheme, in the type of car parks prevalent in the area, and in levels of crime. To take two extremes, car parks operated by NCP Manchester Ltd (NML), no matter how high their quality, are currently unlikely to be submitted for scheme membership, whilst in Canterbury most car parks belong to the scheme. Manchester has a relatively high rate of vehicle crime but this is not the reason behind its lack of involvement in the SCP scheme (most of Manchester city centre's car parks are operated by NCP who have a policy of not putting their car parks forward for SCP awards); Canterbury has a relatively low rate of vehicle crime but in this case, and in line with the flexible nature of SCP awards, this does have some impact on the threshold for car parks to receive the award. Such differences should be borne in mind whilst reading the following analyses.

The first question to be addressed is whether the SCPs in the sample are more highly rated by users than those not part of the scheme and street parking in terms of criteria associated with scheme membership, i.e. lighting, layout, cleanliness, car security and personal safety. To test this, each car park was assigned a score based on summing the ratings of the car parks by users in terms of these characteristics[14]. This produced a score for each site of between five (indicating high levels of concern) and 25 (indicating high levels of satisfaction).

The mean (average) score for SCP car parks, non-SCP car parks and on-street parking are shown in Table 2.2[15]. While the differences are not large they are statistically very significant. One way analysis of variance (ANOVA) and post hoc (Scheffé) tests confirmed that there were very significant differences between each of these means with SCPs being perceived more favourably in these respects than car parks not in the scheme which, in turn, were seen as better than street parking. This pattern held for both multi-storey and surface car parks, though the former received very significantly better ratings than the latter (though again the differences were small).

---

14. The high correlations between these ratings (see table 3.1) suggested that this would be possible. Use of Cronbach's alpha, a measure of the internal reliability of scales, confirmed that adding the ratings together produced a reliable measure (alpha=.81).
15. It should be remembered that the car parks in the sample were not randomly selected from all the SCP and non-SCP car parks in the country. Therefore the results here, as elsewhere, are revealing of the situation in the five case study areas but should not be taken as nationally representative.

Table 2.2: **Mean ratings of car parks**

	Overall	Multi-storey car parks	Surface car parks
SCP car parks (N=832)	19.18	19.29	18.87
Non–SCP car parks (N=573)	18.31	18.53	18.04
On- Street (N=176)	17.07		

Figure 2.2: **Mean ratings of car parks**

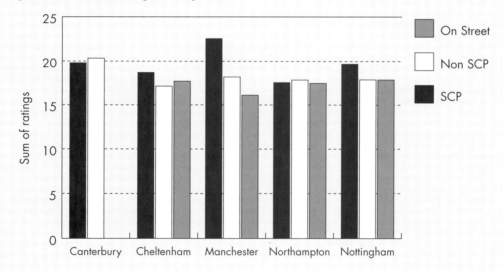

Overall then, the SCPs in the sample are more highly rated by users than car parks not part of the scheme and street parking in terms of the SCP award scheme criteria of lighting, layout, cleanliness, car security and personal safety. As can be seen in Figure 2.2, the pattern varied somewhat from area to area. In three areas, Cheltenham, Manchester and Nottingham, the SCPs are rated as better than the non-SCPs and on- street parking in terms of the criteria being used[16]. In Nottingham and Cheltenham non- SCPs were not viewed

16. Only one SCP was covered by the survey in Manchester (there are only two SCPs in the city centre) and this was the newly constructed Marks & Spencer car park. Many of the other car parks included in the survey are older and it is, therefore, unsurprising that as a whole they were rated lower than the SCP. The non- SCP car parks also exhibited a large range in ratings, with some of the car parks having amongst the lowest ratings but one having the second highest rating in the survey. The car parks in Manchester are also currently undergoing a programme of refurbishment.

more favourably than street parking. Canterbury and Northampton are not in line with the overall pattern. In the former the apparent reversal is due mainly to the low ratings given to a leisure centre car park that has the SCP award. This car park was also rated poorly in the security survey carried out by the independent security consultant. The Northampton findings are less easily explained but they owe something to the relatively poor ratings given to a surface SCP and higher ratings given to a surface car park which is not a member of the scheme (this latter car park is considered locally to have sufficiently high levels of security and low enough crime levels to be made an SCP).

3.   Crime and fear of crime in car parks

This section considers the main factors that appear to control the fear of crime in car parks and compares levels of concern in SCPs to other parking locations. It also looks at the impact of the SCP scheme on levels of vehicle crime. In the final section, we attempt to draw upon these findings in a discussion of the security features that can control levels of crime and fear of crime in car parks.

Fear of crime in car parks

One of the assumptions underpinning the SCP scheme is that, among other things, physical characteristics of car parks have an effect on risk and perceived risk. Questions that can be asked of the survey data are:

- are car parks which are perceived as having the physical characteristics of a Secured Car Park experienced as safer?

- are SCPs perceived as having the characteristics they might be expected to have as members of the scheme?

- does the car-parking public concur with the principles underpinning the SCP scheme in answering the question *what makes a car park safe from crime?*

- what factors control choice of car parks by drivers?

Environmental characteristics and perceived safety

Respondents were asked to rate the place they had parked in terms of several physical characteristics associated with Secured Car Park award scheme status (i.e. cleanliness, lighting and layout) and in terms of car security and their own personal safety. Whether looked at over the whole sample or just for those using car parks, all of these characteristics were significantly positively correlated. Thus, as expected, feelings of security are linked to perceptions of the physical parking environment with cleaner, lighter and better laid-out parking sites being seen as safer, in terms of both car security and personal safety. Table 3.1 shows the correlations[17].

---
17.   For those not familiar with the statistics, stronger relationships are indicated by correlations closer to 1.00 and weaker relationships by correlations closer to zero.

Table 3.1: *Correlations between perceptions of parking site features and feelings of safety*

| | How would you rate the location you parked your car in terms of …. | | | | |
	Cleanliness	Lighting	Layout	Car safety	Personal security
Cleanliness	-	.670	.416	.497	.492
Lighting	.662	-	.473	.485	.470
Layout	.419	.480	-	.377	.393
Car security	.477	.483	.402	-	.900
Personal safety	.463	.465	.417	.900	-

a. Correlations are Pearson product-moment correlations. Those in the top right are for the whole sample; those in italics in the bottom left are for car park users only.
b. N varies for each case because of missing data but all correlations have a probability of p< .001

Further evidence of this comes from the responses to being asked whether they had any worries or concerns about parking in the location they had chosen. Over the sample as a whole there were clear relationships between perceptions of the parking environment and worry (see figure 3.1). Those parked in car parks (16%) were less likely to be worried than those parked on the street (23%) and so the analysis was repeated for car park users only. As can be seen in figure 3.2 the same pattern holds with users of cleaner, better-lit and well laid-out car parks being less worried.

Figure 3.1: *Percentage of whole sample worried or concerned about parking related to perceptions of environmental characteristics of parking site*

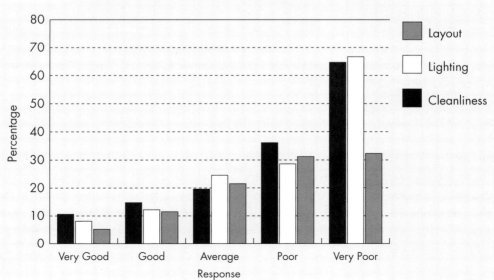

Figure 3.2: *Percentage of car park users worried or concerned about parking related to perceptions of environmental characteristics of parking site*

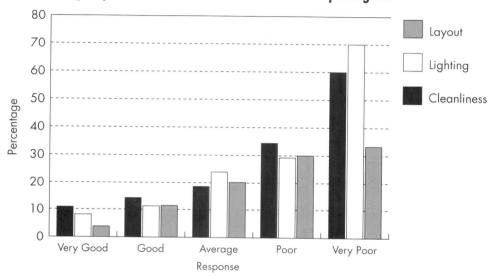

In terms of the public's perceptions of parking places, these findings thus support the emphasis in the SCP scheme on issues of lighting, maintenance and layout.

A related set of questions concerns the relationships between perceptions of the parking environment and concern about being a victim of crime. The relationship between the perceived safety of a car parking spot and concern about crime is likely to be two-way. People who are worried about being victims may be more careful about where they park and choose to park in places they perceive as having characteristics which make them safer. Conversely, anxiety may be affected by the characteristics of the parking site with more anxiety being expressed by those who are parked in environments they perceive as less safe. These two processes would tend to cancel each other out and thus weaken any statistical relationship between worry and the environmental characteristics of parking spots.

However, low but statistically significant or very significant negative correlations were found between these environmental perceptions and concern about victimisation. More concern about being a victim of crime was expressed by those giving less favourable ratings to the parking environment in terms of cleanliness, lighting and layout. These relationships were not very strong though, and thus the environmental perceptions were not very strong[18]

18. For example, the correlation between concern about being a victim of crime in a parking place and the environmental score of that parking place was 0.122, which is highly significant statistically (p<.001, N=1559) but is low.

predictors of concern about victimisation which was more closely related to:

- a general concern about being victimised (in the town centre);

- previous experience of victimisation, with those who had been victims of crime in the previous twelve months expressing more concern;

- gender, with women being more concerned than men; and

- area, with most concern being expressed in higher crime areas and least in lower crime areas e.g .Canterbury parkers were least concerned and Manchester respondents most concerned[19].

Removing (partialling out) the effects of these other variables did increase the strength of the relationships between the perceptions of the qualities of parking sites and concern about victimisation. Overall, the findings suggest that people's concerns about personal victimisation in and around car parks can be affected by these qualities of parking sites but are more a result of such "personal" characteristics as gender, general levels of concern about victimisation, previous victimisation, and of perceptions of risk based on levels of crime. However, as explained above, the possibility that car park choice is *based* on levels of concern needs examining and will be returned to in a later section.

The final issue to be considered here is the response to the question *what makes a car park safe from crime?* The analyses above show that there is a relationship between perceptions of the physical properties of car parks and the extent to which car parks are seen as secure and safe. The SCP scheme though, places stress on other factors apart from these physical characteristics and this question enables us to see whether parkers identify the same characteristics. Respondents were asked, without prompting, what they thought makes car parks safe from crime. They were allowed to give as many answers as they wished and their answers were categorised. Figure 3.3 shows the most common responses.

More than half of the respondents gave answers which emphasised formal surveillance, in the form of patrols and/or involving CCTV, as a key component of a car park safe from crime. The third and fourth most popular responses, good lighting and the presence of other customers, are also concerned with this aspect of security. The popularity of these, together

---

19. These effects tend to be cumulative. For example, of female parkers in Manchester who had been victims of crime in the previous twelve months, nearly three quarters were very or fairly concerned about being a victim of crime either where they had parked or on their way to or from their parking spot. This was true of only 13 per cent of male parkers in Canterbury who had not been victims in the previous twelve months.

with responses which mentioned a lack of 'nooks and crannies', mean that responses concerned with aspects of surveillance make up nearly 78 per cent of all responses to this question. The parking public, then, seems to agree with the emphasis placed on this feature of car parks in the SCP scheme. Some of the other characteristics mentioned in the SCP guidance are perhaps less 'obvious'. It is likely that more people would have picked them out if prompted.

Figure 3.3: *What makes a car park safe from crime?*

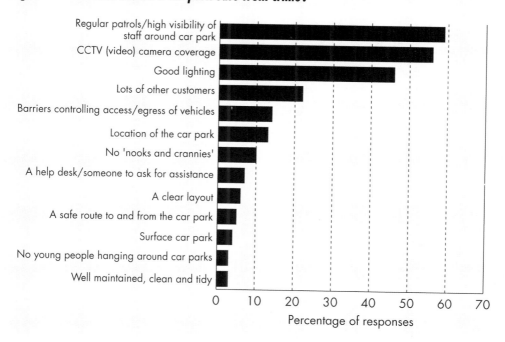

Security and parking choice

The issues surrounding preference are complex. People's preferences (for anything) are based on a multitude of factors, are context-dependent and may vary from one time or place to another, and may not relate closely to actual behaviour. In the course of interviews carried out for this research we did, though, come across views ('theories') that parkers prefer good surface car parks to good multi-storey car parks, that this is especially true of women, and that spending money to make car parks safer is justified by the increased revenue this will attract from an increased number of users. The last of these views is examined in the section on cost-benefits but some survey data also relates to it and the survey did explicitly ask parkers about both their parking preferences and their parking choices.

Stated preference

Respondents were asked where they would prefer to park, if all other things were equal. Nearly a third (32%) said they had no preference while just over half said they would prefer to park in a car park, with roughly equal preferences for surface (28%) and multi-storey (26%) car parks. Fewer than 15 per cent said that they would prefer to park in the street. There were slight but significant differences between males and females in that slightly more men (34%) than women (29%) had no preference and more women (31%) than men (24%) would prefer to park in a surface car park (see Figure 3.4).

Figure 3.4: Where would people prefer to park?

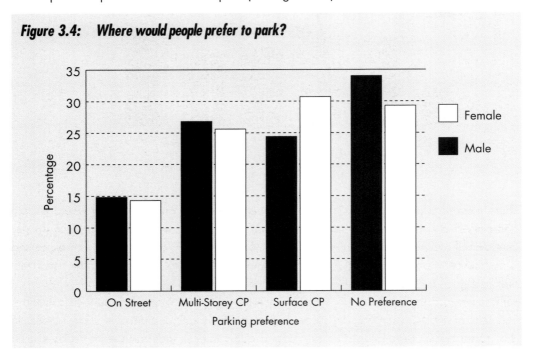

Stated preferences were more markedly affected by how long people were planning to park at the time they were questioned. Figure 3.5 below shows the preferences of those who had a preference against the time they were parking for. Those parking for shorter periods were more likely to say they preferred street parking than were those parking for longer periods. Preference for multi-storey car parks was greatest among those parking for between one and two hours (45% of those who had a preference) while surface car parks were preferred by those parking for between four and six hours (59% of those who had a preference).

Figure 3.5:   Where would people prefer to park by length of parking period?

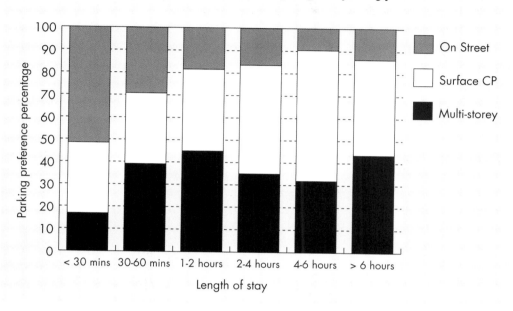

There were also very significant relationships between stated preference and where people had parked and between preference and which town people were parked in. Thus 43 per cent overall preferred the kind of site they were parked in while among those who expressed a preference this rose to 63 per cent. This was especially true of surface car park users with half (50%) of them overall preferring surface car parks and nearly three-quarters (74%) of surface car parkers who had a preference saying they preferred to park in surface car parks. This relationship between parking preference and actual parking choice may be two-way in that some social psychologists have long argued that stated preference *follows* from behaviour, rather than vice-versa, as a means of justifying that behaviour. Thus people's parking preferences may be, to some extent, rationalisations for their parking behaviour.

Parkers in Nottingham and Canterbury were very different in their responses. In the former there was a strong preference for multi-storey car parks (48% of those having a preference) and in the latter a very strong preference for surface car parks (87% of those having a preference). This perhaps results from familiarity and the car parking provision in these two places in that Canterbury has very restricted street car parking and most car parks are surface while, with the exception of park and ride sites outside the city centre, most large car parks in Nottingham are multi-storey. In Manchester there was an overall preference for multi-storey car parks (though there was a difference between men and women with the latter having a slight preference for surface car parks). In Cheltenham and Northampton the patterns were more evenly balanced with a slight preference for surface car parks in the former and for multi-storeys in the latter.

Parking choice

When asked how important various factors were in determining the choice of where they had parked, closeness to destination was identified as important by most respondents with 60 per cent saying it was very important. Safety issues were also identified as important with 45 per cent and 38 per cent saying that the safety of their car and their own personal safety had been very important in choosing where to park. Issues to do with the ease of parking tended to be identified as fairly rather than very important.

Figure 3.6: Factors influencing choice of parking site

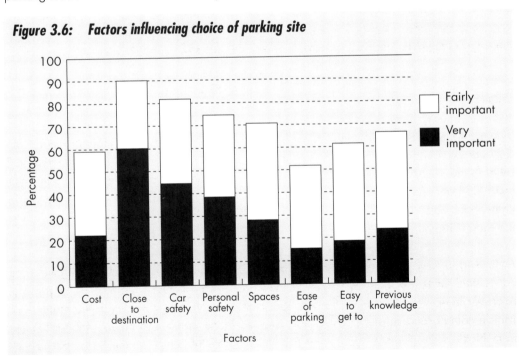

Men and women differed in several of these respects. Most notably, women were more likely than men to say that considerations of personal safety were important in their parking choice with 44 per cent of women saying it was a very important factor compared with 33 per cent of men. Women were also more likely to say (or admit) that ease of parking and manoeuvrability were important to them.

Car park users and street parkers differed in several respects. For example, street parkers were, unsurprisingly, much more likely to emphasise cost as a factor in their parking choice[20] . In contrast, SCP users were more likely than other parkers to stress safety. In relation to car safety, for example, nearly half (49%) of those parked in SCPs said it was very important in determining their choice compared with 40 per cent of those parked in other car parks and 39 per cent of those parked on the street. The corresponding figures for personal safety were 42 per cent, 35 per cent and 34 per cent respectively.

There were no differences between those who had been victims of crime in the previous twelve months and those who had not, but there were significant relationships between fear of crime and the importance placed upon several of these factors. In particular, higher levels of concern about being a victim of crime were associated with placing greater emphasis on both personal safety and car security as factors in parking choice. For example, two thirds of those who were very concerned about being a victim of crime in the town centre said that their own safety or the safety of their car was very important in determining their parking choice.

Crime in car parks

When examining crime in car parks, we have attempted to answer two main questions: *Do SCP car parks have lower levels of crime than other car parks? Does obtaining the SCP award lead to changes in crime?* Crime levels in car parks were compared to those in other local car parks and with crime in the encompassing beat. The significance of variations in crime levels before and after security changes were made to car parks were examined using the *t* Test (Chapter 1, SCP scheme).

According to the British Crime Survey (BCS), car parks account for around 22 per cent of all car related thefts (Kershaw *et al.* 2001). Although the risk of vehicle crime in car parks is relatively high when the length of time parked at a location is considered, the majority of vehicle crime occurs in places other than car parks (Sallybanks and Brown, 1999). Figures from Nottingham, for example, show that the majority of vehicle crime in the city centre occurs to cars parked on streets. There were a total of 489 vehicle crimes in car parks in Nottingham City during 2001 compared with 2,153 crimes against those parked on-street. This is primarily due to the relatively high number of on-street parking spaces in Nottingham compared to car park spaces. In Canterbury, for example, where on-street parking is of much more limited availability, crimes in car parks represent a much higher percentage of the total vehicle crime in the area (but, here too, on-street crime outweighs crime in car parks).

20.   Of street parkers, 36 per cent said cost was very important in their choice of where to park compared with 20 per cent of car park users.

Vehicle crime data from the study areas show that thefts from vehicles were the most common vehicle crimes in car parks; thefts of vehicles, by comparison, are a much smaller problem. For example in Nottingham city centre (Table 3.2), of the 489 reported offences in car parks during 2001, only eleven (2%) were thefts of vehicles (only 5% of reported vehicle thefts in the city centre occurred from car parks, whilst 21% of thefts from vehicles occurred in car parks). Figures for vehicle crime against those parked on-street in the city centre show that, once again, thefts from vehicles was the most common offence (65% of vehicle crime). Thefts of vehicles, however, represents a higher percentage of vehicle crime from on-street parking locations (9%).

Do SCP car parks have lower levels of crime than other car parks?

The SCPs in each of the study areas generally had amongst the lowest levels of car park crime in the particular town or city centre. This is exemplified by Table 3.2, which shows the numbers of reported thefts of and from vehicles in Nottingham city centre car parks during the 2001 calendar year. The car parks in Table 3.2 are arranged in order of increasing number of total offences per 1,000 spaces. This takes account of variations in size of car park but not of usage (usage figures were not available for all of the car parks) or different operating hours.

Table 3.2 reveals that SCP award-bearing car parks (shaded) have some of the lowest crime levels in Nottingham city centre (the crime patterns shown in the table are similar to those seen in previous years). Two car parks, both with the award, had no crime during 2001 (the Victoria Centre White Zone car park has had no reported car crime since it opened in 1997). The table also shows, however, that there are some car parks without the award that have comparable figures to the award car parks both in terms of the annual number of vehicle crimes in the car park and/or crimes per 1,000 spaces. The award-bearing car park at Fletcher Gate, for example, has higher crime levels than the nearby Stoney Street car park, which does not have the award. These car parks are located around 250m apart and are both of similar size but have slightly different opening hours (Stoney Street opens from 7am to midnight and Fletcher Gate from 6.15am to 2.15am). Stoney Street car park is, however, operated by NCP and according to company policy has not been put forward for the award. Fletcher Gate was extensively upgraded prior to receiving its award (including upgrading CCTV and lighting) but crime levels remain relatively high compared to other car parks in Nottingham. The reasons for this are not clear but appear to be related to staffing problems, being targeted by a prolific offender and its use in the evening by people visiting local entertainment facilities. The car park was rated[21] fairly

---

21. See Chapter 2, Security and quality of award car parks for explanation of ratings.

poorly compared with other car parks in Nottingham by users (although had average ratings across the whole sample) but well rated in terms of security by the independent security consultant.

A similar pattern is seen in Northampton, with car parks with SCP awards having amongst the lowest crime levels in the town centre. Two of the car parks, St John's and Grosvenor multi-storey car parks, had no recorded car crime from April 1998 to December 2001. There are, however, two car parks, which are both owned by the local authority, which despite having low vehicle crime levels (and low levels of vehicle crime per 1,000 spaces) do not have SCP awards. One of these car parks, Albion Place, has not been put forward for the award because of the poor condition of the parking surface (the car park's survey ratings – Chapter 2, Security and quality of award car parks – are average and considerably better than those for St John's surface car park which does have the SCP award). The local authority, however, feels that giving this car park the award would impact negatively on the local perceptions of the scheme as a 'quality award'. Grosvenor has not been put forward because of plans to increase the size of the shopping centre that it serves, which would require alterations to the car park (the police also feel that the true crime levels in the car park are not reflected in the recorded crime statistics).

Canterbury is a peculiar example. It has a large number of car parks with SCP awards but also a large number of car parks that the police and local authority consider would get the award but have not yet been put forward because of the rising cost of inspection fees[22]. The car parks without the awards, therefore, have similar levels of both security and crime to the car parks with the awards. For example, the car parks without awards include a newly built park and ride car park that has had no crime since its opening.

The location of a car park is one of the factors that may influence the level of crime. The lower crime levels that on the whole exist in SCPs in both Northampton and Nottingham though cannot be easily explained in terms of just their location. For example, in Nottingham, the Talbot Street car park (SCP award) and Royal Moat House car park (no award) have very different crime levels despite being located on opposite sides of the same street (both are multi-storey car parks of similar size; Table 3.2). An examination of the various car parks at the out-of-town retail centre at Leicester's Fosse Park (Box 3.1), which are all located on the same site also suggests that factors other than location are controlling the variation in crime levels (Table 3.3).

---

22. The standard inspection fee is £150 a year but discounts can be negotiated with the British Parking Association for operators who have multiple car parks on the ACPO scheme.

Table 3.2: Reported car crime in Nottingham city centre car parks 2001

CAR PARK	Parking spaces	Type	Theft from vehicles	Theft of vehicles	Damage	Vehicle interference	Total	Car crime per space
Victoria Centre (White Zone)	1066	MS	0	0	0	0	0	0.0
Talbot Street	590	MS	0	0	0	0	0	0.0
Forest Park and Ride	3000	S	8	0	0	3	11	3.7
Victoria Centre (Main)	1700	MS	7	0	0	2	9	5.3
Trinity Square	335	MS	0	1	1	1	3	9.0
Broadmarsh Centre	1200	MS	19	1	1	2	23	19.2
Wollaton St GNCS	125	MS	1	0	0	2	3	24.0
Stoney St	600	MS	13	0	0	2	15	25.0
Mount Street	425	MS	13	0	1	3	17	40.0
Fletcher Gate	550	MS	19	1	1	5	26	47.3
Curzon Street	167	S	6	1	1	1	9	53.9
Arndale	412	MS	25	0	1	0	26	63.1
St James St	475	MS	31	1	1	4	37	77.9
Sneinton Market	50	S	6	0	0	1	7	140.0
Royal Moat House Hotel	625	MS	78	0	8	17	103	164.8
Europa PS	225	MS	37	0	1	1	39	173.3
Brook Street	56	S	16	0	0	7	23	410.7
Gill Street	49	S	14	2	1	6	23	469.4
Huntingdon Street	75	S	34	2	1	4	41	546.7

Car parks that held a Secured Car Park award during 2001 are shown unshaded. S=Surface car park; MS=multi-storey car park.

Table 3.3:   Vehicle crime at the Fosse Park site

		Fosse Park	Supermarket 1	Supermarket 2	Hotel
1998/99	TFMV	4	1	5	23
	TOMV	2	2	8	2
	CD	1	1	4	12
1999/00	TFMV	0	2	3	23
	TOMV	1	0	6	2
	CD	3	3	2	16
2000/01	TFMV	0	1	9	26
	TOMV	1	4	1	4
	CD	4	1	3	9

TFMV = Thefts from motor vehicles, TOMV = Thefts of motor vehicles, CD= Criminal damage to vehicles

Box 3.1:   Vehicle crime at Fosse Park, Leicester

Fosse Park retail centre is served by two car parks (south site and main site), with two supermarket car parks and a hotel car park on the same site. The south site (the smaller of two car parks) commenced operating in 1997 and received an SCP award in 1998 (no work was required to bring this site up to standard). The main site, which has been in operation since 1989, achieved the award in 1999, with only a small amount of work required to meet SCP standards (higher specification of bulbs in lighting, external phone lines and signage). Security is primarily provided by 22 CCTV cameras and physical patrols. Every shift has a four-man team, with two people monitoring the CCTV screens and two physically patrolling the car parks, roles are regularly switched to avoid boredom and fatigue. All patrol staff have high visibility jackets and caps (which the operators suggest makes customers feel more secure and is good for staff morale), all carry radios with panic alarms. Crime levels in the car park are low, particularly when compared with the car parks attached to two different supermarket chains and a much smaller car park serving a hotel (Table 3.3). The hotel, which largely serves businesspeople, has particularly high crime levels compared to other local car parks.

The low crime levels of the Fosse Park car park are attributed locally to the good surveillance provided both by the patrols and the CCTV system. The effective management practices and commitment to customer satisfaction are also noticeable features at the site[23]. The retail park management team also suggests that *"our reputation acts as a deterrent to would-be offenders, on both shoplifters and car crime"*. It is noticeable that the car park is not

---

23.   The evaluators had first-hand experience of the effectiveness of the security: we were stopped by security staff within minutes of arriving for an unannounced visit after the CCTV operators had observed one of our party photographing the car park.

surrounded by perimeter fencing, which would limit the ease of access to and from the shops in the retail park. The car park is, however, surrounded by fields, which in the eyes of the local police beat officer reduces the need for fencing the car park. There are, however, barriers to all access and egress points on both car parks. High crime levels in the hotel car park are possibly related to the availability of suitable targets (e.g. *"laptops left in the back of cars"*) and also possibly to the fact that cars are left in the hotel car park for longer lengths of time (including overnight stays). Fosse Park and the two supermarkets are also members of the local Car Park Watch Scheme (Box 5.1).

Does obtaining the SCP award lead to reductions in car crime?

Identifying the impact of achieving the SCP award is often difficult because:

- before-and-after data is not available for those car parks that are built to Secured Car Park award scheme specifications (e.g. the Victoria Centre White Zone car park in Nottingham);

- there are difficulties in assigning a cut-off date to use in an analysis of before-and-after changes in car crime. For example, car park improvements may occur over a number of years or, in other cases, very little (or nothing) has to be done to get the award and consequently there are no large changes in security;

- some car parks have been members of the award scheme for many years and historic data is not readily available for these car parks. For example, the Broadmarsh Centre car park in Nottingham was a member of the original award scheme (pre-1996); and

- there are a range of additional factors that can impact on the levels of vehicle crime in the car parks. For example, other police or partnership initiatives to tackle vehicle crime, changes in parking regulations within the city, changes in the level of usage of car parks.

The majority of SCPs are either new car parks built to achieve the award (e.g. Victoria Centre White Zone car park; Chapter 4, Cost-effectiveness study 2) or ones that required little alteration (e.g. Fosse Park). The targeting of car parks that required little improvement was encouraged by the setting of a target to reach 2000 award car parks by the year 2000. It has been suggested that this target served to concentrate attention (and money) away from those car parks that needed the most attention. There are, however, a small number of higher crime car parks where the SCP award has been targeted as a method of reducing crime levels.

Although based upon a small number of examples, evidence from the study areas shows that car parks built to become SCPs have low (sometimes zero) crime levels. Car parks with pre-existing low crime levels, particularly where few changes take place, do not generally show significant reductions on becoming SCPs. Reductions in vehicle crime can, however, occur when higher crime car parks are targeted for improvement. A series of case studies are presented to illustrate these points.

In a small number of cases, however, crime levels rose following the receipt of an SCP award. The increases in vehicle crime levels in these cases were, however, low and not statistically significant.

Case study 1: Northampton

The first four local authority car parks in Northampton to become SCPs were selected because they required little modification and already had relatively low crime levels (Figure 3.7)[24]. For example, one (St John's multi-storey) had experienced no recorded vehicle crime prior to the award (going back to at least April 1998) and has remained crime-free since. The car parks included three surface car parks (St Peter's Way, Commercial Street and St John's surface) and one multi-storey car park (St John's multi-storey) and they received their award in December 1999.

---

24. One of the car parks, St John's surface, received one of the lowest ratings of surveyed car parks (Chapter 2, Security and Quality of award car parks). The survey was, however, conducted at the start of 2001, some time after the initial decision to put the car park forward for an SCP award was taken. The security consultant did not feel that there were any major causes for concern at the site.

Figure 3.7: **Crime levels on St Peter's Way, Commercial Street, St John's surface and St John's multi-storey car parks**

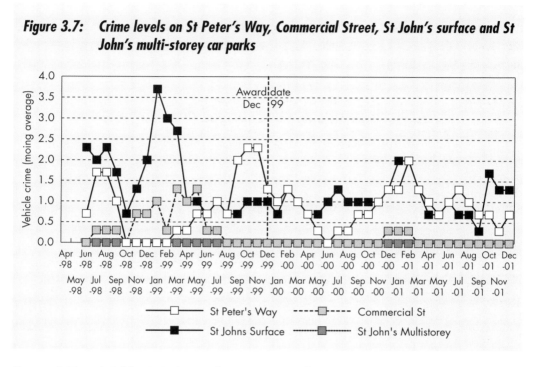

Figure 3.7 and Table 3.4 shows that Commercial Street experienced very significant decreases in crime following receipt of its award but that crime in the other car parks did not change significantly. Furthermore, the level of vehicle crime in the car park as a percentage of that in the enclosing beat did not greatly alter over this time period. There is no clear link between usage and crime levels (the car parks were all well used prior to receiving the SCP award) but it is possible that the increases in usage of some of the car parks was partly as a result to the improvements to the car parks (Table 3.4), which the local authority believes occurred at Commercial Street. The decreased usage of St John's multi-storey immediately following the award may be due to increased usage of the adjacent St John's surface car park.

Very significant decreases in vehicle crime were recorded in other car parks in Northampton over the same time period. In particular, large decreases were seen at St James' Retail Park (down 21), Wellington Street (down 10), Nene Valley (down 10) and Mayorhold car parks (down 8). The reductions at Mayorhold car park largely followed the receipt of its SCP award in August 2000 and reductions at Wellington Street car park are possibly related to the increased coverage of the town centre's CCTV camera system. CCTV coverage was also installed at Nene Valley retail site (and two of the main businesses that were attracting crime at the site closed down). Although vehicle crime reduced at St James'

Retail Park, levels still remained relatively high[25]. Significant reductions in vehicle crime were also seen in the police beats in which the car parks are situated, possibly as a result of the increased CCTV coverage in the town centre.

Table 3.4: **Statistical significance of changes in crime and usage in the Twelve-months before and after the award in Northampton (December 1999)**

	Crime change[26]	Usage change	Vehicle crime in car park as % of vehicle crime in beat	
			Pre	Post
St John's multi-storey	Not significant	Very significant decrease	<1%	<1%
St John's surface	Not significant	Very significant increase	2.5%	2.3%
St Peter's Way	Not significant	Not significant	<1%	<1%
Commercial St	Very significant, but small, decrease	Very significant increase	<1%	<1%

Figure 3.8: **Crime levels at the Mayorhold, Ridings and St Michael's car parks**

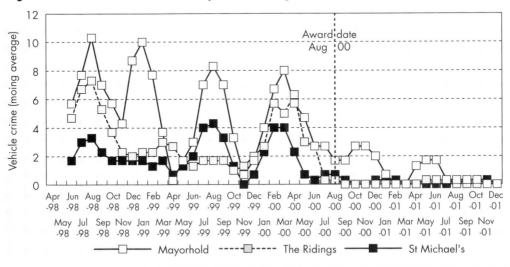

25.	Security improvements at this site are now under way.

26.	Vehicle crime at St Peter's Way car park fell from eleven offences in the twelve-months prior to the award to nine offences in the following twelve-months. Crime in St John's surface car park fell from 17 to twelve offences over the same time period (mainly due to a reduction in thefts of vehicles, which fell from five to two; thefts from motor vehicles actually increased by one). Crime levels at Commercial Street reduced from five vehicle crimes in the twelve-months prior to receipt of the award to zero in the year after.

The evidence, therefore, suggests that the receipt of the SCP award by the four car parks did not greatly affect their levels of vehicle crime (the small reductions at Commercial Street car park cannot confidently be attributed to the effect of gaining SCP status since beat crime also reduced over the same time period and the ratio of crime in the car park to crime in the police beat did not alter). However, it did serve to generate interest amongst local councillors in obtaining the award (they appreciated the good publicity and kudos associated with getting the award). This led to a commitment to upgrade further car parks to award status (this is written into the local Crime and Disorder Strategy and Community Plan). The next three car parks were selected because of their relatively high crime levels compared with other local authority car parks. Two multi-storey car parks (Mayorhold and St Michael's) were selected along with one surface car park (The Ridings). All three received their awards in August 2000.

Figure 3.8 and Table 3.5 show that vehicle crime levels in the three car parks reduced very significantly following receipt of the award and have remained at this reduced level. Very significant reductions were, however, also recorded in other non-award bearing car parks in Northampton over the same time period[27] but no significant reductions were seen in the beats in which the three car parks are situated.

Table 3.5: Changes in crime and usage in the twelve-months before and after the award in Northampton (August 2000)

	Crime change	Usage change	Vehicle crime in car park as % of vehicle crime in beat	
			Pre	Post
Mayorhold	Very significant decrease	Not significant	5%	2%
The Ridings	Very significant decrease	Significant increase	5%	<1%
St Michael's	Very significant decrease	Not significant	3%	<1%

The only significant variation in usage amongst the three car parks was seen at The Ridings, where usage increased significantly after receipt of the award. Variation in usage does not, therefore, appear to be a large factor in the change in crime levels. The increased usage of

27. The police suggest that this corresponds to the arrest of one prolific offender that used to target one particular car park near his home. Improvements to Victoria Promenade car park occurred at a similar time to those in the study car parks and involved the installation of CCTV, the pruning of shrubbery and general refurbishment, which appeared to lead to reductions in crime at the site.

The Ridings is attributed by the local authority to increased night-time parking. Following receipt of the award, the local authority introduced a night-time charge and encouraged people to use this, and other SCPs, on the grounds that they offered a safer place to park at night.

In addition, the local police report a reduction in incidents of disorder on The Ridings following the improvements. This car park is situated close to a number of pubs and clubs and, before it was upgraded, the car park was a location for prostitution and drug taking (making discarded needles a frequent hazard). Such incidents have, reportedly, also reduced after the car park was upgraded.

The evidence supports the suggestion that the vehicle crime reductions at these car parks were largely due to the security alterations that took place. The improvements mainly involved installation of CCTV cameras and improved signage (as was the case at all car parks in Northampton that became SCPs). Where necessary, lighting levels were also improved (e.g. The Ridings car park) and some minor pruning of shrubbery was also required at some car parks (e.g. Commercial Street).

Case study 2: Canterbury

Fourteen car parks in Canterbury currently have SCP awards. Most already had low crime levels and minimal alteration was required before their award. Examination of three such car parks that received their award in July 1999 revealed no significant reductions in crime. Vehicle crime at one of the car parks (Longport surface car park) actually increased slightly from one crime in the twelve-months prior to receipt of the award to five in the following twelve-months (this change is not, however, statistically significant). Longport was not put forward for re-inspection in the following year due to a problem with street drinkers using the car park (Box 3.2).

Box 3.2: Canterbury

Longport car park

Longport surface car park in Canterbury first received an SCP award in July 1999. The car park was not, however, put forward by the council for re-inspection the following year because of a problem with street drinkers using the car park. Some instances of car park users being harassed at the payment machines were reported.

The problem was remedied by using a number of approaches: the car park has been re-designed and 45 per cent of the car park is now used as a coach drop-off point (with an attendant), street furniture was removed to take away places for the drinkers to sit on, shrubbery was tidied up, a city centre by-law which prevents on-street drinking was extended to cover the car park and local off-licences were targeted by the police licensing officer.

Castle Street car park

Prior to receiving an SCP award in July 1999, the layout of the car park was redesigned and the car park redecorated. Changes included alteration of the circulation system, marking of pedestrian walkways and weatherproofing of the top deck (the number of spaces was reduced from 538 to 466 spaces to allow these changes to take place). New lighting and CCTV were also installed immediately prior to receiving the award.

The alteration of the circulatory system improved natural surveillance and also helped to remove 'dead zones' (areas with no frequent through traffic).

Castle Street car park in Canterbury, which also received its award in July 1999, however, required a significant programme of improvements prior to receiving its award (Box 3.2). The car park had relatively high levels of crime (compared with other local car parks) prior to its refurbishment. Vehicle crime reduced very significantly from 36 crimes in the year prior to the award to five in the following twelve-month period. The car park accounted for 31 per cent of vehicle crime on the beat in the year up to July 1999 but for only 6 per cent of beat crime in the following twelve-months. This suggests that, although crime in the beat fell very significantly over the same time period, the crime reductions in the car park are significant in the context of local crime patterns (the reductions in vehicle crime in the car park may have contributed to the reductions in beat level vehicle crime).

Case study 3: Derby

Bold Lane car park in Derby offers another example of where a relatively high-crime car park has been targeted for improvement. The car park is run as a partnership between Parksafe (Systems) Ltd and Derby City Council and is notable for both the technical innovation that has gone into the design of the car park (Box 3.3) and the reductions in crime which this has led to. Prior to its renovation, the car park had the highest level of vehicle crime in Derby with 95 thefts from vehicles and twelve thefts of vehicles during the 1996/97 financial year (the car park accounted for a quarter of all thefts from vehicles that occurred in the city centre's 14 public car parks). The car park also had problems with vandalism, aggressive beggars and street drinkers. The car park had remained a crime hotspot despite installation of CCTV cameras and improvement to the lighting. The renovated car park began operation in January 1998 and has had no crime[28] or incidents of anti-social behaviour since this time. Car park usage increased by 23 per cent in the year after refurbishment despite increasing the cost of parking to 20 pence an hour more than other car parks (much of this has been due to increased night-time usage of the car park).

Box 3.3: Bold Lane car park, Derby

Bold Lane car park began operating after undergoing a major refurbishment in January 1998 at a cost of £0.5 million. The multi-storey car park was built in the late 1960s and has 440 spaces. Prior to the refurbishment, the car park had serious problems with vehicle crime and forms of anti-social behaviour.

The security system encompasses individual motion sensors in each parking bay, panic buttons at 15 meter intervals on the parking decks and landings, 200 automated CCTV cameras, pedestrian – proof vehicle entry/exit gates and separate ticket entry-only pedestrian access. The car park guarantees the safety of customers' cars and their contents and has taken out full public liability insurance through Lloyds of London to back this guarantee.

The equipment and systems installed at Bold Lane won the British Parking Association's Quality in Action Award for Best Practice in Parking in 1998. Parksafe's customer guarantee was also given an innovation award at the 2002 British Parking Awards. A user survey conducted by the City Council in 2000 showed that 97 per cent of users felt personally safe using the car park, 100 per cent felt that their car and contents were secure in the car park and 89 per cent said that the car park represented good (51%) or excellent (38%) value for money. The car park was formerly a member of the SCP award scheme but has since withdrawn its membership.

---

28. Compared with 78 vehicle crimes in the previous twelve-month period before January 1998.

Case study 4: Changes over time

Figure 3.9: *Crime levels in a shopping centre and hotel car parks*

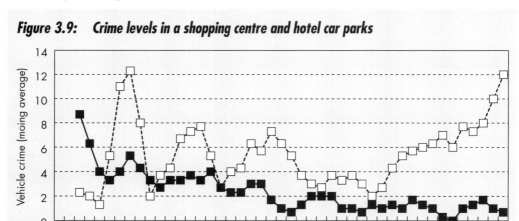

Upgrading the security of a car park to achieve the SCP award can take a number of years. Some operators, for example, choose to carry out staged improvements over a number of financial years. It may be anticipated that crime levels reduce in such car parks as the level of security improves. This assumption is, in part, supported by the findings from the following case study.

Two multi-storey car parks, located approximately 0.5km apart on the northern edge of a city's main shopping area were examined. One of the car parks serves a shopping centre and is the larger of the two. The other serves, but not exclusively, a hotel. The operators of both car parks have been upgrading the car parks over a number of years, with the stated aim of achieving the SCP award.

Figure 3.9 shows that whilst crime in the shopping centre car park has reduced over time, car crime in the hotel car park, after showing some initial reductions, rose during 2001. The shopping centre car park received its award in December 2001, whilst the hotel car park is unlikely to achieve the award[29] in the near future.

The shopping centre underwent a substantial programme of improvements, which included upgrading lighting and CCTV, painting, signage, installation of reflective sheeting to walls and

---

29.   Despite this, the car park advertises on a local radio station that it offers secure parking.

general refurbishment. Improving the car park required a substantial financial investment, which reflects the management's determination to achieve the award and their strong focus on customer satisfaction. Money is also available to allow for on-going maintenance and repairs to be made and the management is constantly looking for ways to improve the car park.

The lack of comparable success at the hotel car park is largely due to insufficient resources being made available to carry out the necessary improvements, despite a desire at local level to achieve SCP. Whereas financial decisions at the shopping centre are made locally, decisions at the hotel are largely made centrally at the head office of the hotel chain. For example, hotel staff members were used to paint the car park rather than bringing in external contractors (the increased surveillance generated as the painting took place temporarily appeared to reduce crime levels in the car park) and, although CCTV cameras were installed and lighting upgraded, the improvements were of a lower standard than those suggested by the hotel staff and local ALO. Despite the lack of success, one positive feature is that the ALO has managed to at least generate a local interest at the hotel in achieving SCP status. Improving the car park is now, therefore, given a higher priority by the hotel than before.

Reducing crime and fear of crime in car parks

The previous section provides evidence that vehicle crime levels can reduce significantly in car parks after they become SCPs (although there are exceptions, such as car parks with very low, pre-existing, crime levels where crime remained low and a few examples where crime levels actually increased[30]) and that car parks built to SCP standard have low crime levels. The key measures that impact on both crime levels and fear of crime appear to be surveillance, lighting, access control and the physical appearance of the car park. The possible deterrent value of the SCP award seems to be of less importance. These measures are discussed further in this chapter.

In Northampton, the reduction in crime levels at St Michael's, The Ridings and Mayorhold car parks were locally attributed to the introduction of CCTV cameras at the sites (this was the main change to take place at the sites). The installation of CCTV was believed to be particularly important at The Ridings and St Michael's car parks because both had little natural surveillance (The Ridings car park is *"tucked away at the back of town"* and St Michael's is a long-stay car park used by town centre workers meaning that *"you don't see anybody after 10am in the morning and only the odd car in the evenings"*). This lack of natural surveillance was believed to be the main contributing factor to the crime levels in these two car parks.

---

30. These increases were not, however, statistically significant.

Castle Street multi-storey car park underwent a range of improvements prior to achieving an SCP award, leading to a significant reduction in levels of vehicle crime (case study 2). This is attributed locally to the improved surveillance of the site through both the CCTV and alteration to the circulation system (both supported by improved lighting). It was also suggested that these alterations had the positive crime prevention effect of increasing natural surveillance and appears to have largely displaced the young people who previously congregated within the car park.

As noted in Chapter 2, Security and quality of awarded car parks, the installation of CCTV is one of the most common approaches to obtain an SCP award. These examples suggest that this emphasis on CCTV is justified. The crime reductions at Bold Lane car park and low crime levels at Fosse Park, both of which rely heavily on CCTV as part of their security system, also lend support to this view. The survey of car park users revealed a belief amongst respondents that CCTV camera coverage makes a car park safer from crime. CCTV could, therefore, also impact on the fear of crime. These findings are consistent with those of other evaluations of the effectiveness of CCTV in car parks (e.g. Poyner, 1997; Tilley, 1993; Welsh and Farrington, 2002 and in other locations – e.g. Brown, 1995. For example, Welsh and Farrington, 2002 concluded that the most reliable findings on the effectiveness of CCTV came from studies in car parks, where CCTV was found to have contributed to a 45 per cent reduction in vehicle crime overall.

In most cases, improvements to lighting went alongside improvements to CCTV systems. Improvements to lighting were often described as being essential to support the functionality of the CCTV system, to help prevent offenders from concealing themselves from view and improve natural surveillance. It is, therefore, difficult to separate the effects of the two. Good levels of lighting were also considered important for reducing the fear of crime. The survey results support this view, with users suggesting that good lighting makes a car park safe from crime. Good lighting was shown to be a key factor in determining a quality car park in a survey of users of multi-storey car parks (Connaught, 1998). Smith (1996) presents case studies from New York and San Diego, where crime levels in car parks were apparently reduced by installing effective lighting systems. The effect of lighting has also been shown to have positive crime prevention effects in other settings (e.g. Painter and Farrington, 1997; Painter and Farrington, 2001; Welsh and Farrington, 2002).

The survey showed that regular patrols/high visibility of staff around car parks was the highest scoring response to the question, "what makes car parks safe from crime?" Regular car park controls are a key security feature at Fosse Park retail park, where they are used in conjunction with the CCTV system (the CCTV controllers can direct the patrolling officers to specific incidents or areas). Whilst the retail park is a low-crime, well managed car park, it is hard to say with certainty what impact the patrols have had as distinct to that of the CCTV system (or the combined effects of both, or other features). The security patrols do, however, add to the feeling of a high security presence at the site. In Manchester, patrols form an important part of the security system (Box 3.4). Patrols are targeted at any car parks where problems are occurring. Patrols are seen by the car parks' management as the most effective way of tackling crime problems and reducing the fear of crime (see also Moster and Longmore-Etheridge, 2000). The customer relation benefits of having a high staff presence in car parks was also stressed by NML and other operators (in addition to crime problems, for example, they can respond to problems with ticket machines and other queries). Some car parks had staff members overlooking the entrance/exit to the car park (such as Talbot Street, Nottingham; Bold Lane, Derby; and High Street, Manchester). These car parks have low crime levels and most are rated highly by customers. The increased presence of staff in a hotel car park during refurbishment (case study 4) appeared to have had an impact on crime levels. Other evaluations have also indicated that guards and attendants in car parks can be effective (e.g. Webb et al., 1992; Poyner, 1997; Laycock and Austin, 1992; Barclay et al., 1996[31]; McDonagh et al., 2002).

Sturry Road in Canterbury (described later) provides an example of where directed police patrols appear to have led to a reduction in vehicle crime. Eck and Spellman (1992) also report on the successful use of directed police patrols to reduce the number of thefts from motor vehicles in large, surface, shipyard car parks in Virginia, USA.

Some of the study areas have parking attendants that patrol car parks, primarily enforcing parking regulations. Although they could possibly play a role in preventing crime, the small amount of time that they spend in each car park, and lack of emphasis from management of their role in reducing crime, appears to mean that this role is very limited. In the Beechwood car park in Cheltenham, which was highly rated by the security consultant, high profile staff patrols were augmented by the cleaning staff, who operate with specific instructions concerning security matters.

---

31. In Barclay et al.'s study, security patrols took place on bicycles. This allowed the patrols to get around the large parking lots faster (and therefore pass each point more regularly), increased their visibility and gave the patrols a slightly higher vantage point. Patrols on mountain bikes have also recently been introduced at a shopping centre at Crawley, West Sussex (Parking News, 2002). Staff at Fletcher Gate and Broadmarsh car parks in Nottingham use electric buggies for patrolling.

Box 3.4: NML Manchester

NCP Manchester Ltd (NML) is a partnership between NCP and Manchester City Council and operates a large percentage of Manchester's city centre car parks. The partnership was seen as the solution to the City Council's problem of having insufficient money to carry out the necessary improvements to its parking stock. Under the partnership arrangements, NML leases both the City Council's and NCP's city centre car parks. A substantial refurbishment of the car parks is under way and the centrepiece of the development is the construction of a new control room. The local police were not invited to provide design advice during the construction of the car parks or building of the control centre but are supportive of the developments. A requirement to tackle crime within the car parks was, however, included within the partnership agreement. It is too soon to comment on the impact on crime levels of the car park improvements in Manchester, but information provided by NCP for its Cardiff control room reveals large reductions in vehicle crime in Cardiff's car parks since the control room began operation in August 1999.

The new control room has been built at a cost of £3.1 million. Digital CCTV images from 312 car park cameras, covering 50 car parks, are displayed on 162 monitors. The room is also used to monitor the City Council's 79 city centre cameras; these are monitored by staff employed by the City Council. Images are stored on hard drives with 50 terabytes of storage. The control room also houses Manchester's Retail Crime Operations Manager and the City Council's CCTV Project Manager, which emphasises the joined-up, partnership approach. The control room also services three local security radio networks. A police position has also been built in the control room to allow a police officer to monitor the images. This position also has Automatic Number Plate Recognition (ANPR) and facial recognition system capabilities (these facilities are only available to the police). The control room began operating in January 2002 but has not, at the time of writing, had its official opening. Discussions with the police to have an officer manning the police position for 18 hours a day are on-going. In addition, around £10 million is being spent on upgrading the specification of car parks, which includes improved lighting, help points that link to the control room and general refurbishment work. The NML car parks have all received ISO certification and follow NCP's nation-wide management practices. Similar control rooms, though based on analogue systems, have been developed in Leicester, Birmingham, Cardiff and Bristol.

The building of the control room and introduction of new ticket machines has meant that staff who were previously deployed in kiosks, and whose main function was issuing tickets and taking payments, can now be used for patrolling. The control room allows NML to adopt a 'Smart Manning' approach. Car parks that are more susceptible to crime, or that have had a recent spate of car crime, can be identified from the NCP's BROMAT[32] system and discussion with the police. Extra staff can then be deployed in these car parks, whilst monitoring of the car parks with lower risk can be prioritised by the CCTV operators. The company argues that visible staff patrols are the best deterrent to crime and also help to minimise fear of crime. The control room and associated systems have crime prevention benefits but also allows NML to monitor car park machinery, staff for health and safety reasons and also to help deter staff fraud. NML also expects that customer satisfaction will increase because of the increased patrolling within the car parks.

None of the car parks that are operated by NML have the Secured Car Park award. Several would not qualify for the award because of a lack of some of the security measures required by the award and some were rated relatively low in the survey of users. Many would, however, be eligible for the award but have not been put forward for the award in accordance with current NCP policy. Representatives from NML, however, argue that by spending money on the control room and adopting a largely management-focused approach to reducing crime, with an emphasis on working in partnership and problem-solving, they have developed a more cost-effective mechanism for preventing crime than if they had upgraded the security features of each car park to gain SCP awards. The focus on partnership working and problem solving is not, however, unique to Manchester's car parks and is a feature of many areas with SCPs; some of which are also managed from central control rooms (although Manchester's control room does stand out in terms of the technologies employed and the integrated nature of its operation). The improvements made to Manchester's car parks were still on-going at the end of 2001 and the effectiveness of the control room and other improvements to car park security need to be evaluated, and compared to the successes that the SCP award scheme has had in reducing crime, before conclusions can be drawn about the relative merits of this approach.

Most of the car parks in the study areas had good levels of natural surveillance, even those that were rated poorly by users or had relatively high crime rates. In some cases, the good natural surveillance was as a result of poor perimeter treatment (e.g. the site was open, allowing surveillance from the street but without any access control). The worst sites, however, generally had poor formal surveillance suggesting that car parks should not rely only on high levels of natural surveillance to overcome the lack of formal surveillance.

32. See Box 5.2.

Access control is a key component of the SCP award. As noted above, the use of perimeter fencing varied considerably between areas, with some surface car parks having no perimeter fence. There was, however, generally some attempt to reduce the ease of exiting the car park other than through the allowed exits (e.g. through the use of shrubbery or sloping banks) at all sites. Perimeter fencing was not installed in any of the car parks in the study areas we visited to obtain the SCP award[33] (or more generally prevent crime) and, therefore, we cannot comment on its effect on reducing crime levels.

There is some evidence, however, to suggest that controlled access to car parks can assist in preventing vehicle crime. A problem with vehicle crime, especially thefts from vehicles developed at Sturry Road Park-and-Ride car park in Canterbury in 1998/99. In response, barrier– controlled access to the site was introduced, manning levels were also altered at the same time to ensure that staff were always on-site during opening hours (this was partly to make sure that there was somebody to respond to any problems with the barriers) and the police targeted the site with patrols. The local authority and police suggest that the police patrols had an immediate impact on crime problems and the barriers ensured that these reductions in crime were maintained. Problems with the crime data for this car park, however, prevent this assertion from being tested[34]. Sturry Road car park does not currently have an SCP award but, according to the local police, following the improvements described it would now be eligible to receive an award. Controlled access is also a key element of a number of the multi-storey car parks in the study areas, such as the Bold Lane car park (Box 3.3). Evidence presented by Poyner (1997) also suggests that controlled access to car parks can help to reduce crime.

At many car parks, such as Castle Street in Canterbury, improvements to the general appearance and layout of the car park occurred at the same time as security improvements. The survey showed that there is a relationship between perceptions of physical properties of car parks (such as cleanliness, layout and lighting) and the extent to which car parks are seen as secure and safe. It would, therefore, seem plausible that such improvements could send out the same signals to would-be offenders and the improvements to the physical properties of car parks could, therefore, act as a deterrent. The effect that littering, vandalism and loitering can have in town centres on attracting potential offenders and deterring legitimate users has been recognised by some authors (Wilson and Kelling, 1982; URBED, 1994).

---

33. Car parks, which were built to SCP standard, did include perimeter fencing but this did not allow the effectiveness of perimeter fencing on its own to be evaluated.

34. Recorded police vehicle crime figures for the period when the problems were occurring show very little crime in the car park. It was suggested locally that this may be due to problems in the allocating of crime to the car park. Crime levels in the car park prior to the interventions were estimated to be in the order of 50 thefts from motor vehicles during 1998/99 with several thefts of motor vehicles. This reduced to five thefts from motor vehicles in 1999/2000 and six in 2000/01, with no thefts of motor vehicles in either year.

One possible theory is that crime reductions are due to publicity surrounding the granting of the award (or the awareness that improvements are being made). Other evaluations of crime prevention initiatives have shown that publicising initiatives can lead to reductions in crime (e.g. Laycock, 1992; Barclay et al., 1997). However, public awareness of the scheme is relatively low (Chapter 2, Security and quality of award car parks) and reductions in crime are evident in areas where successful achievement of SCP awards is not advertised (eg Canterbury). Although the value of publicity should not be ignored, the sustained reductions in crime at some sites (and the low crime levels at new-builds) tends to support the view that the reductions are directly due to the improved security measures. In some areas, such as Northampton, it is possible that there was some dispersion of benefits to other car parks (in this case, the spread of CCTV coverage across the town centre is also likely to have had an effect on vehicle crime levels).

4.   Costs and benefits

Introduction

Off-street parking generates a considerable amount of money, with the 29 largest private operators in the UK each having turnovers of over £1 million and profits amounting to a total of over £65million (Parking Review, 2001)[35]. Parking provision is also an important source of employment, with these major private operators alone employing around 10,000 staff to run their off-street parking operations (Parking Review, 2001). One survey showed that the average motorist uses a multi-storey car park twice a week spending up to £5 per week, £250 a year (Connaught, 1998). Research commissioned by Friends of the Earth in 1998 showed that the typical English surface local authority car park run by a local authority of 108 spaces yielded an annual income of £35,424 (£328 per space) and a typical multi-storey (543 spaces) yielded £189,507 (£349 per space) (ETRA, 1998).

The Road Traffic Regulation Act (1984) allows local authorities to retain money from parking charges to spend on transport issues. Specifically section 55 (4) states that any surpluses should be used to provide or maintain off-street parking accommodation unless this is *"unnecessary or undesirable"* (in which case funding must be targeted towards other transport issues as specified in the Act). A review of local authority parking revenues[36] in London for 2001/02 revealed revenues ranging from £448,717 in Hillingdon to £62,742,131 in Westminster (Lydall, 2002). The average (median) revenue per London borough was around £2.5m. Such surpluses offer a potential source of funding improvements to car parks to SCP standard. However, whilst the review noted that parking surpluses were being used "for the public good", it noted that surpluses were routinely being used in part for improvements that were not directly related to transport services (Evening Standard, 2002).

Decisions to upgrade car parks, or to apply for an SCP award, are generally taken after a consideration of the costs and benefits associated with the task. For example, a Home Office telephone survey revealed that the 68 per cent of local authority contacts that did not have any award-bearing car parks said that this was because the level of investment required was too high (WCJ, 1999a; WCJ 1999b). Inspections and re-inspections under the SCP award scheme

---

35. Many parking operators also offer other services, such as enforcement of on-street parking regulations, and figures, therefore, do not represent turnover or profits solely from the provision of off-street parking services.
36. Figures include car parks and residents' parking permits. In some cases, annual figures were estimated and figures for one London borough (Havering) were not available.

currently cost car park operators £150 annually per car park (although discounts are available for multi-site operators where a number of inspections can be arranged on the same day). The cost of upgrading car parks to achieve the award varies considerably depending upon the initial quality of the car park (it is generally easier, for example, to upgrade a surface car park rather than a multi-storey to award standard[37]). For example, some car parks may only need to make minor cosmetic changes to achieve the award, such as pruning shrubbery, and hence costs will be negligible but others may have to make major structural changes, install new CCTV or lighting, etc. which could cost several hundred thousand pounds or more. Providing security can also incur on-going costs. For example, one out-of-town retail site that we examined estimated annual staff costs (17 dedicated car park staff including security, maintenance, and secretarial personnel and six management staff) of approximately £350,000 and CCTV rental costs of £35,000 (including maintenance). The benefits of running an attractive, well used site, as the profit figures described show, can however be considerable. This is further exemplified by the example of Castle Street car park in Canterbury, where both usage and profits increased following improvements to the car parks (despite a loss of 72 parking spaces as a result of the improvements)[38]. There is also some evidence that usage in some of Northampton's car parks may have increased as a result of improvements to the car parks.

Profits from parking charges are not, however, the only driver for improving car parks. For example, some car parks with the SCP award are free to park in. In the case of Daventry District Council, the decision to invest in improving the town's car parks was largely taken on the basis that it would potentially attract more visitors to the town and, therefore, have a positive impact on the town's overall economy. The car park has been described as the 'gateway' to a town and can immediately engender a positive, or otherwise, image of the town in the visitor (a similar argument could be applied to large shopping centres or retail parks).

Local authorities are also encouraged to upgrade their car parks through the best value process (e.g. Audit Commission, 2000). The Audit Commission and the Improvement and Development Agency have jointly created a library of local performance indicators (PIs) for use by local authorities, which includes the PI: *"Percentage of car parking covered by a Secured Car Park award"*. Northampton Borough Council commented about the SCP award that *"it is very useful in a cash-strapped council to have a badge. The public are often critical of the services they get after paying their taxes, so it is nice to have a tangible argument against costs – we can show the public what we have done with their money"*.

---

37. Two-thirds of ALOs surveyed at the 2001 ALO's conference in Blackpool agreed with the statement that, "it is easier to improve a surface car park to award standard than a multi-storey car park".

38. Council estimates suggest that the usage of the car park increased from 211,478 a year in 1998/99 (which is similar to the previous year's figure) to over 240,000 in both of the following two financial years. It has been suggested that the increased usage is as a result of the improvements to the appearance of the car park, which itself has increased natural surveillance of the car park.

Section 17 of the Crime and Disorder Act (1998) is another potential driver for improving security in car parks. This section imposes a duty on each local authority to *"exercise its functions with due regard to... the need to do all it reasonably can to prevent crime and disorder in its area"*. Failure to carry out this duty could lead to a local authority being challenged by judicial review (Moss and Pease, 1999). In his letter to chief executives of local authorities in 1999, which was designed to encourage membership of the SCP award scheme, the Home Office Minister Paul Boateng emphasised that, *"this means that decisions about the provision and management of local authority car parks must now be taken against a crime and disorder background"*. Manchester City Council ensured that security in car parks was a condition of the contract that was established with NCP when setting up NCP Manchester Limited (NML).

Two sites in the English Midlands were selected to allow a detailed examination of the costs and benefits of upgrading the security of car parks. The study examined car parks owned by a local authority at one site and car parks operated by a property company at the other, making use of the methodology set out in the Home Office guide to assessing the economic and social costs of crime (Brand and Price, 2000).

Cost effectiveness Study 1: municipal by owned and operated car parks

Two car parks in Northampton, St John's surface car park and The Ridings multi-storey car park, were selected for detailed analysis. The local authorities at both county and district levels and the police service have a long history of effective partnership to improve community safety. An important element in these multi-agency partnerships has been one of the UK's leading schemes for closed-circuit television (CCTV) across the town centre. Cameras covering the town centre, the public car parks and retail-and other private sector organisations such as public houses – are linked together under the supervision of a control centre manned on a 24-hour basis. Officers of the District Council believed that raising the standards of all the town centre car parks to a level corresponding to SCP status would provide significant benefits. These were:

- parking itself would be safer and more secure, with fewer losses to car owners from theft of and from vehicles, or damage to vehicles; and

- because car parks would be perceived by car owners as more attractive, clean, brighter and more secure they would be used more, bringing benefits of:

  ❑ additional revenue from parking charges

❏ less congestion with its attendant costs, caused by on-street parking

❏ more business for town centre retail and leisure activities, leading to better profits for the operators.

The officers of the local council had first to convince the councillors that the investment to achieve SCP status would be worthwhile. They therefore chose a pilot project to upgrade one car park which required comparatively little work to be done to meet the SCP standards, with correspondingly limited investment. Through this pilot project the town gained experience in how the SCP scheme worked; there was also further improvement in the relations between the District Council officers and the police; favourable publicity for the District Council was generated by achievement of the SCP status and presentation of the award by the Chief Constable.

As a consequence of the results achieved through the pilot programme, councillors agreed to a progressive development programme to upgrade, where necessary, its municipally owned and operated car parks to meet the SCP standards. In a separate but related project, a scheme for automatic number plate recognition has been implemented, linked both to the national vehicle licensing system and the police national computer system.

The particular project chosen for this cost effectiveness evaluation is St John's surface car park. This car park is situated adjacent to the St John's multi-storey car park, and has a capacity of 160 vehicle spaces compared with the 600 vehicle spaces of the multi-storey car park. The car park received its award of SCP status in December 1999 and vehicle crime has declined noticeably. The work needed to achieve SCP status for this car park was only relatively minor, as appropriate lighting and CCTV coverage were already in place, with CCTV integrated into the town centre-wide scheme. The improvement needed therefore was concentrated on signing and minor improvements in perimeter security. This is the pilot project which led to further development of the SCP scheme in the town.

In 1998/99 St John's surface car park experienced 26 criminal incidents, including ten of motor vehicle theft. By contrast, the total number of vehicle crimes in 1999/2000 was ten and in 2000/2001 fourteen (of which six cases were criminal damage to vehicles including three in January 2001). St John's surface car park is situated in police beat BNN12, which has seen a decline of 24 per cent of vehicle crime over the last three years. Vehicle interference over the last three years has dropped by 49 per cent; theft of motor vehicles has decreased by 30 per cent and thefts from motor vehicles have reduced by 27 per cent. Criminal damage to vehicles has increased very slightly – up by three per cent.

These figures must be seen in the general context of the overall decline of vehicle crime in the town and the considerable efforts which, as noted, have been devoted to maintaining and improving community safety in the town as a whole through the use of the town centre CCTV system and broader community safety partnership. Overall vehicle crime has decreased in the town by 17 per cent over the past two years, with only criminal damage to vehicles showing a slight increase – up by three per cent. The greatest reductions have been in aggravated vehicle taking, which has fallen by 36 per cent from 55 incidents in 1998/99 to 35 incidents in 2000/01. Vehicle interference has reduced by 23 per cent, theft from vehicles by 21 per cent and theft of vehicles by 19 per cent.

The measures taken in the St John's surface car park, with which this cost effectiveness evaluation is concerned, have, it can be argued, made their own contribution to improvement in the wider context of the town's measures against car crime. It is therefore not appropriate to scale down any assessment of effects of the changes made to secure SCP status on the grounds that "car crime has been declining generally".

From the figures given it may be seen that in the particular instance of St John's surface car park there does not seem to have been any great decline in thefts from motor vehicles. But thefts of motor vehicles have declined from ten per annum to a level of one per annum and criminal damage/interference has declined from ten incidents per annum to six incidents per annum.

Apart from annual re-inspection costs of the SCP award (£150 – say £500 to include the costs of time for District Council officers operating the scheme), annual operating costs are insignificant: as the CCTV and management costs are already integrated with the overall town centre scheme and have not been increased, or decreased, significantly due to SCP status.

Recognising the additional security that SCP standards underpin, evening charges have been introduced, and car park use has increased. It is estimated that the increased revenue attributable to the achievement of SCP standards is some £33,338. Other than the evening charge, parking charges have not been increased.

In short, the cost-effectiveness analysis shows that each of the different interests has benefited from the achievement of SCP standards for this car park: for users the cost of loss and damage to vehicles has been reduced by an amount equivalent to £0.27 per user. For the operator, the local authority, there has been an improvement in the total of operating and amortised capital costs of an amount equivalent to £0.24 per user; and there has been a reduction in the costs to the criminal justice system of an amount equivalent to £0.005per user. The relevant figures, and their derivation, are summarised in Table A.1.

In contrast to the St John's surface car park, The Ridings car park, also a surface car park in the town centre, has required some significant investment in improved lighting and CCTV provision to upgrade to meet SCP standards. SCP status was awarded to The Ridings car park in autumn 2001, and as a result of the upgrading, significant benefits have arisen in terms of:

- reduction in vehicle crime;

- increase in income to district council through the ability to increase charges including a night-time charge; and

- reduction in offences such as vandalism, and prostitution which were previously a problem in the area.

Improved conditions and perceived good value for users is generating more visits by shoppers and this in turn is increasing the prosperity of the shops and businesses in the area. Less on-street parking and traffic congestion is also a consequence of the improved use of this car park.

The Ridings car park is situated in the centre of the town in an area where there are a number of pubs and clubs. Before it was upgraded, the car park was a location for prostitution and drug taking, making discarded needles a frequent hazard. The upgrading which resulted in The Ridings car park receiving SCP status was completed in June 2001. The Ridings car park has 60 parking spaces and some 88,000 users per annum. Since July 2001 crime in The Ridings car park has reduced by the equivalent of: 2 incidents per annum of theft of vehicles; 22 incidents per annum of theft from vehicles; and five incidents per annum of criminal damage/interference.

There has also been a reduction in vandalism to street furniture such as signs and ticketing machines, giving a saving of £4,000 per annum. Improved conditions now enable the council to make a 50p evening charge for parking in the car park, which is yielding an increased annual income of £40,000.

The work required to improve the car park to SCP standards included:

- installation of one additional CCTV camera at a cost of £1,500 per annum; and

- improved signage and access control, together with general repairs to the fabric – at a cost of £20,300.

As in the case of the St John's surface car park there are also the costs of renewing the SCP award – say £500 per annum, to include the town's own administrative costs.

Again, the cost-effectiveness analysis shows that each of the different interests has benefited from the achievement of SCP standards for this car park: for users the cost of loss and damage to vehicles has been reduced by an amount equivalent to £0.23 per user; for the operator, the local authority, there has been an improvement in the total of operating and amortised capital costs of an amount equivalent to £0.45 per user; and there has been a reduction in the costs of the criminal justice system of an amount equivalent to £0.24 per user. The relevant figures, and their derivation, are summarised in Table A.2.

Cost-effectiveness study 2: city centre car park serving a shopping centre owned and operated by a property company

The new Nottingham-based Victoria Centre White Zone multi-storey car park is an integral part of the retail shopping centre located on the site previously occupied by one of the two city centre railway stations in a major midland city. The property company originally involved in the development of the site has continued in an active involvement with the shopping centre as landlord and operator. It is one of a small number of major centres in the city and offers users a wide range of shops, restaurants etc. under cover and with readily accessible car parking.

A considerable effort is made to ensure that the appearance of the centre and the opportunities it provides are kept up-to-date in a way which will appeal to the users. This is with the aim of maximising the number of users of the centre, and the amount they spend during their visits. The company's policies for operating the centre are designed to promote a "virtuous circle" of:

- high standards leading to customer confidence; which in turn leads to

- greater flow of customers to the shopping centre; this in turn leads to

- more turnover and better profits for the tenants of the centre; this leads to

- more demand from tenants for space, with the expectation of high standards of provision and operation; which leads in turn to

- fewer shorter voids and better rentals for the centre operating company.

The company sees the standards governing the design, construction, operations and maintenance of the centre car park in this context.

The original Victoria Centre had been developed in 1972 on the site of the previous Victoria Railway Station. In the late 1990s it was decided to extend the centre considerably to create a new shopping mall, using the adjacent site of the old city bus station. This new development of the Victoria Centre included the creation of a new bus station and a new car park, each with under- cover pedestrian access to the shopping mall. The design brief for the new White Zone car park was based on acceptance that it should meet the SCP standard. This decision follows from surveys of customers of the original Victoria Centre car park. The surveys had found that women, in particular, felt threatened by the underground nature and relative darkness of older car parks. The design of the White Zone car park, therefore, incorporated from the beginning:

- high standards of painting;

- high standards of lighting;

- pay station at the lift lobby covered clearly by CCTV;

- CCTV coverage of the parking area; and

- good visibility within the parking area.

Operational policies have included keeping a high standard of cleanliness and maintenance, ensuring that staff have a smart uniform and are very visible as they go about their duties. The pricing policy adopted for the car park is to match, or to be slightly below, the price for parking in the city's municipally owned city centre car parks, and follows the city's pricing for whole day "parking". Whole day parking is restricted because it tends to attract office workers and others who are not frequent users of the centre.

Overall crime in the city has shown little change over the last three years with only a three per cent reduction in the two years between 1998/99 and 2000/01. Although there has been a noticeable drop in aggravated vehicle taking (24%) theft of vehicles (16%) and criminal damage to vehicles (14%) during this period, there has been an increase in vehicle interference which is up by a third (33%).

The White Zone car park has 1,100 spaces. It operates on a 24-hour basis and has been crime- free since it came into operation in 1997. Usage of the car park has risen by over 10 per cent each year since 1997. It continues to be crime-free, having experienced no vehicle crime at all in the last three years. The neighbouring old Victoria Centre car park also had significant reductions in the level of vehicle crime over the last two years. In 1998/99 a total of 59 crimes were recorded in that car park, which includes 53 incidents of theft from vehicles. Between 1998/99 and 2000/01 these figures reduced by over 70 per cent. In 2000/01 there were no incidents of theft of motor vehicles or criminal damage and the number of thefts from motor vehicles fell by 14 per cent.

The beat that includes these two car parks has seen 14 per cent more vehicle crime over the same period of time. There has been a 6 per cent drop in theft of motor vehicles and 12 per cent decrease in criminal damage to motor vehicles in the beat, but there has been a 16 per cent increase in theft from motor vehicles and a 146 per cent increase in motor vehicle interference. Theft of vehicles constitutes the largest portion of the cost of crime to vehicle owners and the changes in theft of vehicles are to some extent counterbalanced by the offences of theft from vehicles and interference. It might therefore be appropriate to regard the change in the level of crime in the surrounding area outside the centre as of relatively little significance to any assessment of the cost-effectiveness of the standards of design and operation of the Victoria Centre car parks.

As there has been no reported crime in the White Zone car park since it opened, how should its effectiveness be assessed? It may be considered appropriate to regard the benefits, in terms of the reduction in crime levels resulting from the standards of design and operation achieved in the new car park, as equivalent to a reduction to zero in all the three categories of criminal incidents, theft of vehicles, theft from vehicles and criminal damage/interference, from a level proportionate to that experienced in the old Victoria Centre car park before the programme of improvements there was put in hand (in 1998/99).

The additional benefits to the car park operator flowing from higher user confidence, to greater use of the car park, higher footfall in the mall, and hence higher rentals, would be difficult to assess in isolation from other design and operational matters: which include general improvement in the design and operations of the mall itself. As an example, an increase in parking revenues of one per cent would generate additional income of approximately £12,000 per annum: but on the assumption that the average spend per visit for each user of the car park is some £25, a one per cent increase in turnover for the centre as a whole, deriving from car park users' would be worth approximately £140,000 per annum.

The costs appropriate to the higher standards of design and operation achieved in the White Zone car park, rather than providing a "bare minimum" standard have been estimated through discussion with the management of the centre as representing some five per cent of the total construction costs of the car park. The resulting estimate is a total of approximately £200,000 in relation to initial construction and capital costs. The additional costs of continuing operation for painting, cleaning and other equipment, lighting, CCTV provision, staffing and cleaning, and costs of re-inspection for renewal of SCP status are estimated at some £100,000 per annum.

The cost-effectiveness analysis shows that the achievement of SCP standards for this car park has resulted in a reduction in the cost of loss and damage to vehicles for users, of an amount equivalent to £0.09 per user, and a reduction in the costs of the criminal justice system, of an amount equivalent to £0.004 per user. For the operator, a marginal increase in the total of operating and amortised capital costs (an amount equivalent to £0.004 per user) is almost certainly outweighed by the benefits to the operator of significant increases in the number of users of the shopping facilities the car park serves. The relevant figures, and their derivation, are summarised in Table A.3.

At first the utilisation of the new car park was lower than that of the old Victoria Centre car park. Over the four years in which the new car park has been open. There has been a gradual change and the new car park has increased its utilisation and now fills before the old car park. The old car park has 1,700 spaces and is open from 8am until 10.30pm. Following on from the success of the White Zone car park and the refurbishment of the older parts of the shopping centre, a decision was taken to upgrade the old car park to meet the SCP standards and the old Victoria Centre car park was awarded SCP status in December 2001.

The reduction in crime incidents in the old Victoria Centre car park attributable to the higher standards represented by SCP status can therefore be regarded as a reduction from the levels experienced in 1998/9. That is, six thefts of vehicles, 53 thefts from vehicles and ten incidents of criminal damage/interference. SCP status was awarded in December 2001 and recognises the standards that have been achieved. It may therefore be appropriate to regard the crime levels experienced in the year leading up to that date as representative of the continuing situation. That is: no incidents of theft of vehicles, and a reduction to, at the most, 40 per cent of the previous levels of theft from vehicles and criminal damage/interference.

As in the case of the new White Zone car park, the additional benefits to the car park operator flowing from higher user confidence to greater use of the car park, higher footfall in the mall, and hence higher rentals would be difficult to assess in isolation from other design and operational matters, which include general improvement in the design and operations of the mall itself. However, as an example an increase in parking revenues of one per cent would generate additional income of £15,000: and, on the assumption that the average spend per visit for each user of the car park is some £25, a one per cent increase in turnover, deriving from car park users would be worth approximately £150,000 per annum.

The costs appropriate to the higher standards of design and operation achieved in the old Victoria Centre car park, rather than those evident previously have, again, been estimated through discussion with the management of the centre. The resulting estimate is a total of £200,000 of capital costs for refurbishment. Additional costs of continuing operation for painting, cleaning and other equipment, lighting, CCTV provision, staffing and cleaning, and costs of re-inspection for renewal of SCP status are estimated at some £130,000 per annum

In this case, too, the cost-effectiveness analysis shows that the achievement of SCP standards for this car park has resulted in a reduction in the cost of loss and damage to vehicles for users, of an amount equivalent to £0.07 per user, and a reduction in the costs of the criminal justice system of an amount equivalent to £0.002 per user. Again, a marginal increase in the operator's total of operating and amortised capital costs (an amount equivalent to £0.012 per user) is almost certainly outweighed by the benefits to the operator of significant increases in the number of users of the shopping facilities the car park serves. The relevant figures, and their derivation, are summarised in Table A.4.

5.   Conclusions

Introduction

The Secured Car Park Award Scheme is nearly ten years old. There are currently just over 1,000 car parks in England and Wales with awards (out of an estimated total of 20,000[39]). The number of SCPs has been growing at a steady rate since the new scheme was introduced in November 1997 (Figure 2.1) but membership levels have increased unevenly across the country. Take-up has been particularly low in some urban areas, where vehicle crime levels are relatively high. Public awareness of the scheme remains low (less than one in five car users in our survey had heard of the scheme).

There is evidence to suggest that the award scheme can help reduce the level of vehicle crime and fear of crime in car parks, when targeted at high-crime car parks. Furthermore, some new car parks are built to incorporate high levels of security, sometimes with the aim of achieving an SCP award, and these tend to deliver very low crime levels and be highly rated by users. Spin-offs of the award scheme include increased partnership working between the police and car park operators and a greater emphasis on car park security in some areas. Similar close working was also, however, seen in other areas, such as Manchester. Our study also shows that although crime levels in car parks can be substantial, a greater volume of crime often occurs against cars parked on the street. Thefts from vehicles in car parks is much more common than thefts of vehicles.

What measures help to reduce crime and fear of crime in car parks?

Formal surveillance (including patrols), lighting, access control and a good physical appearance of the car park can lead to reductions in car crime (or maintain low crime levels in newly built car parks). These features are also those shown by our survey to be important in helping to reduce the fear of crime (e.g. Figure 3.3). The survey showed that cleaner, lighter and better laid-out parking sites are seen as safer by the public, in terms of both security and personal safety, and that those parked in such car parks were less worried about parking than those parked in other locations. Environmental factors were also shown to have an impact on levels of concern about being a victim of crime. This impact was,

---

39.   It is not, however, clear how many of these car parks would realistically be able to be targeted by the scheme in the foreseeable future since, for example, the figure includes many small car parks attached to public houses, churches, schools, etc.

however, low and concern about victimisation was shown to be more closely related to general concerns about being victimised, previous experience of victimisation, gender (women were more concerned) and the overall crime rate of the area. A study of car park users in Cardiff revealed similar results with users identifying a range of environmental factors that increase anxiety when parking (Nelson, 1997). The features that were most commonly cited in this study as raising anxiety were blind spots, dark/shadowy areas, poor lighting and payment areas. A range of other environmental features were also identified including graffiti, lack of maintenance and odour, as well as lack of visible staff (Nelson, 1997).

The car parks that were most highly rated in the survey were all relatively new multi-storey car parks and all had low levels of vehicle crime. Three of these car parks had an SCP award and the fourth was a car park operated by NCP Manchester Ltd. This would perhaps suggest that new car parks are being built to a higher design specification and this may in part be due to the standards set by the SCP award (and an increase in knowledge of what constitutes a 'good', safe car park). These car parks tend to have both CCTV coverage and staff present on site. In addition, the car parks tend to be well maintained, be clean and light and incorporate other features such as good manoeuvrability in and out of spaces, marked pedestrian walkways, etc. Some of these are not criteria for obtaining an SCP award but do appear to have an impact on reducing fear of crime and on perhaps reducing crime levels. This has led some operators to suggest that the SCP award should become an overall 'quality' award; similar, for example, to the 'star ratings' given to hotels.

The car parks with the lowest user ratings were all old surface car parks (one of these was an SCP). Crime levels in these car parks were usually higher than in better ranked surface car parks (although one, which primarily served office workers and opened only between 7am and 7pm on weekdays, had low crime levels). They tend to be lacking in formal surveillance and have poorly defined perimeters. It is not possible to say that one type of car park has less crime than others: our results show that there are both high and low crime surface and multi-storey car parks (although the very lowest levels of crime were seen in new multi-storey car parks).

It is generally recognised that it is easier to build-in security from the outset rather than modify car parks at a later stage. In some cases, the scheme's guidance manual has been used by car park developers in new developments thereby ensuring that good design features are built-in from the start. Evidence from car parks such as the main Victoria Centre car park in Nottingham does, however, show that intrinsic design flaws can be overcome. It is also recognised that it is generally easier, and less expensive to upgrade surface car parks than old multi-storey car parks, which may have implications for the spread of the scheme.

Management of car parks

In line with the criteria for membership of the SCP scheme, the management of car parks appears to be a critical factor in developing safer car parks. Those car parks that rank highly in terms of public ratings, crime levels and the views of the independent security adviser tend to be particularly well managed and place a strong emphasis on customer satisfaction. They also generally have a greater level of financial investment and place a greater emphasis on issues such as staff training. Management practices play an important role in the effectiveness of security systems. For example, we have already given one example where the evaluators were quickly stopped in a car park when acting suspiciously (photographing the security features). In another car park, however, both the evaluators and the security consultant (on more than one occasion) were able to walk around a multi-storey car park unchallenged (the security consultant even closely examined the CCTV cameras to check their mountings but was still not stopped). In another case, we were informed that exit barriers are removed at busy times in an airport car park to reduce waiting times at the exit. Good security can be undermined by poor management practices.

The scheme's self-assessment guidance manual

The impact that the scheme's self assessment guidance manual has had on improving general standards of security in car parks is difficult to measure. It appears, however, that the manual has often been used as a source of reference and ideas even in those cases where car park operators have decided not to apply for an award. The manual was also rated highly by ALOs attending their 2001 annual conference[40] and the measures advocated in the manual relate closely to the factors shown to affect levels of crime and fear of crime in car parks.

Variations in security standards

The standard of security in SCPs varies considerably across the country. This is to be expected, to some degree, given the risk-commensurate nature of the award scheme. Some of the levels of security seen in low-crime areas would not be acceptable in higher crime areas. This can make it easier (and less expensive) for car parks in lower crime areas to obtain the award, which could have implications for the broadening of the scheme.

---

40. For example, 80 per cent agreed with the statement that, "the self-assessment questionnaire is a useful tool when conducting assessments" and 63 per cent agreed that, "the manual acts as 'the bible' for the SCP award scheme".

Some of the variation in standards, however, appears to be due to the inconsistent application of the scheme's criteria. One police officer, for example, suggested that he may allow a car park with relatively low levels of security to get an award, so that he can use this as a lever to insist that the car park carries out further improvements the following year to keep the award. Similarly, another suggested that if an operator disputed the need for a particular security improvement, he would possibly allow the operator the benefit of the doubt, but on the understanding that if crime did occur in the car park then the measure would have to be introduced before obtaining the award in the following year. These are understandably pragmatic approaches but add weight to the view that some car parks with SCP awards do not deserve them (Chapter 2, Security and quality in award car parks). However, whilst security standards did vary, awards tend to be given to car parks that delivered low crime levels (e.g. Table 3.2).

The car parking business is very competitive and, given the cost of upgrading car parks, the inconsistent application impacts on operators and their views of the scheme. For example, we were told of one example where an operator who had invested heavily to upgrade his car park to gain an SCP award complained about another local car park having the award because, in his view, the security standards were much lower. Different application of the scheme between areas can also lead to confusion amongst those responsible for constructing or operating car parks in different parts of the country. Furthermore, the inconsistent application of the scheme has important implications for the advertising of the scheme to the public. What can the public expect from a car park with the SCP award?

Costs and benefits

The cost of upgrading a car park (or building a new one) can be considerable and the level of investment required can be a barrier to an operator adopting the scheme (see for example WCJ, 1999a and 1999b). Expenditure is also required to repair, clean and maintain car parks to keep them at a high standard (such regular expenditure is a feature of better car parks in the study). There is, however, evidence to suggest that improvements to car parks can lead to both increased usage and profits for operators (such as was seen, for example, at Castle Street car park in Canterbury, some of Northampton's car parks and Bold Lane, Derby). Increased car park usage can lead to increased usage of other related services or facilities, which can bring additional benefits for operators, such as increased revenue from rental charges in a shopping centre. Usage and profits, however, are not likely to increase where the car park was previously being well used, which can make it difficult to encourage operators to improve security in such circumstances.

In some areas, such as Northampton, the award process has acted as an effective driver to improving car park security. Daventry Council also sees benefits in obtaining the award to encourage visitors to the town. Others though, have suggested that the relatively low public awareness of the scheme reduces the commercial advantages of displaying the SCP signage. In areas such as Manchester, car park security has improved without direct influence of the award scheme. Bold Lane car park in Derby provides an example where financial considerations and previous experience of the owner (Davey *et al.*, 2001) acted as the drivers for improving security (the sort of technical innovation seen at Bold Lane is not, however, encouraged by the award scheme.)

The impact of the scheme has been limited by the relatively low take-up of the scheme. Furthermore, the common practice of targeting scheme membership towards low-crime car parks that require little improvement has meant that vehicle crime is not reduced in many cases as a result of the award process (though the example from Northampton shows that this can be an important step in gaining impetus for the award scheme in an area). The importance of the award scheme in reducing crime is likely to increase if both the number of award scheme car parks and public awareness of the scheme increase (the two are likely to go hand-in-hand). Increased public awareness of the scheme may mean that motorists begin to look for SCPs when choosing somewhere to park, which would possibly stimulate other car park operators to upgrade their car parks. However, the survey showed that proximity to destination is the most important factor that controls choice of parking location and there may be difficulties in trying to persuade owners of well-used car parks to upgrade their levels of security.

Other approaches to reducing crime in car parks

In addition to the measures contained within the award scheme, in the course of our evaluation we have come across a number of other measures that offer proven or promising ways of reducing crime in car parks (Box 5.1). Not all of these approaches have, however, been researched and evaluated. For example, in some areas we are aware that car parks have introduced car washers, who move about the car park and wash cars in-situ to increase natural surveillance in the car park[41] and provide an additional service to customers. Several police officers suggested that vehicle crime levels can be greatly influenced by the presence of one or two prolific offenders and that imprisoning such prolific offenders can have a large effect on vehicle crime levels[42]. This is partly supported by the experiences in Birmingham described in Box 8 and the arrest of a prolific offender was described as a possible cause of the reduction in crime in a car park in Northampton (Chapter 3, Crime in car parks).

41.　In some car parks, for example, the Broadmarsh Centre in Nottingham, cars are left to be cleaned in a separate part of the car park. This, however, eliminates the informal patrolling function associated with other washing schemes.
42.　See, for example, Slobodian and Browne (2001) and Light et al. (1993) for a discussion of vehicle crime perpetrators.

A selection of approaches is presented in Box 5.1. Some of the examples described in Box 5.1 could easily run alongside the current award scheme (although many require independent evaluation of their effectiveness). For example, part of the award criteria could require car park operators to provide evidence of working in partnership with other local agencies or provide evidence that they have run a certain number of targeted crime prevention initiatives in their car park during the year (where this is warranted). Another approach could be to encourage groups of SCP car parks in an area to adopt a Car Park Watch Scheme such as the one in Leicestershire (5.1).

Box 5.1: Examples of other approaches

Parksafe

The Parksafe System, which is described in Box 3.3, led to large reductions in crime in a previously high crime car park in Derby. The system was developed through the inventiveness of Parksafe's owner and as a response to his own experience of crime in a car park (Davey et al., 2001). Such technological advancements are not actively encouraged through the SCP Award Scheme but are recognised by the Annual British Parking Awards. John Heasman, Director General of the British Parking Association. suggests that whilst there has been a gradual increase in the level of technology used, *"because 80 per cent of car parks are owned by local authorities, but may be managed by companies, there is no great competition or incentive. Consequently development and implementation of high-tech features for car parks is slow"* (quoted in Wraige, 2001).

Car Park Watch Scheme

Leicester's Car Park Watch Scheme includes Fosse Park Retail Park and two nearby supermarkets (Box 3.1), a leisure park, business park and local hospitals. Members of the scheme, which has been operating since 1997, meet four times a year to discuss problems with the local police and, at each of these meetings, the police distribute pictures of three known, active, car criminals for members to be aware of. All members of the scheme have pagers to alert each other about 'suspicious' cars and occupants. Local figures suggest that crime in car parks within the scheme has reduced by 36 per cent (this reduction cannot, however, be confidently solely attributed to the scheme). Some scheme members also have the Secured Car Park award.

NML Manchester

A new digital control room has been built, which also houses the city centre's CCTV control room (Box 3.4).

Anti-Social Behaviour Orders

The NCP has worked in partnership with the police and local authority in Birmingham to secure ASBOs against two well-known car thieves. The first person, Matthew, had been arrested on twelve previous occasions and was thought to be responsible for at least 70 offences. The NCP was able to identify 24 occasions on which he had entered NCP car parks during a four-month period, despite not owning a vehicle. Matthew was made subject of an ASBO in August 2000, shortly after completing an eight-month prison sentence, which banned him from entering the city centre car parks. In January 2001, NCP staff observed him entering a car park and he was later arrested and sentenced to a six-month prison sentence for breaching the order. After his release, he was spotted once more in an NCP car park and received another six-month custodial sentence. The second person, Leon, was sentenced to three months imprisonment after breaching his ASBO and he is currently awaiting trial after a further breach of his order. Incident figures provided by the NCP reveal large reductions in vehicle crime during the time that Matthew and Leon were serving custodial sentences and NCP's Security Controller commented, *"although the order does not seem to deter these particular two, I am convinced that it does deter others and at least we get a respite from them when they are in prison"*.

Targeted initiatives and patrols

Car park staff and police in Manchester took part in a Christmas anti-car park crime campaign over Christmas 2001. During Operation Yuletide, customers were handed crime prevention leaflets on arriving at the car park and there were also high visibility visits to the car parks by the police. Information provided by the NCP shows that crime in the last quarter of 2001 was 21 per cent lower than in the previous year. A Christmas operation was also run in Glasgow, with additional patrols by the police and NCP staff, with NCP figures showing a 20 per cent reduction in crime in the last quarter of 2001 compared with the previous year. Information from Sturry Road in this study and other studies (e.g. Eckman and Spellman, 1992) show the benefits of targeting patrols in hotspot areas.

Automated parking

Autosafe, the UK's first fully automated car park, opened in Edinburgh in November 2001. The Sky Parks system allows cars to be vertically stacked on racks using computer-controlled robotics and takes up only half the space of a conventional multi-storey. There is no public access to the building beyond the second level and public areas are safeguarded with CCTV surveillance. The chief operating officer suggests *"insurance* premiums are lower because cars parked in automated spaces are less susceptible to theft and damage" (Parking News, 2002b). A semi-automatic system at Rochester Row car park has also been in operation in Westminster for over 30 years (Building, 1968) and, since the public does not have access to the car park, has had no crime since it opened in 1968. An evaluation of automated parking systems in Italy, which included a consideration of safety/security issues, revealed "exceptionally high patron acceptance and ease of use" (CERF, 2001). Webb et al. (1992) also discusses the benefits of automated stacking car parks in preventing car crime.

Automatic Number Plate Recognition (ANPR)

CCTV cameras in Northampton have had the capability for ANPR (see, for example, Parking Today, 2000) since April 2001. The local police believe that this has had a big impact on general crime levels in the town. Although this does not directly prevent vehicle crime occurring in a particular car park, it has been suggested that such systems can contribute to the overall reduction of vehicle crime in car parks and elsewhere. ANPR technology (and facial recognition capabilities) has also been built into the new CCTV control room in Manchester.

Conclusions

One senior police officer queried whether or not the existence of the award scheme adds something in addition to other crime prevention mechanisms. For example, would it be just as effective for ACPO to issue guidance on car park security that ALOs, planners and car park operators could refer to when necessary? Would Crime and Disorder Reduction Partnerships, as part of their work, target high-crime car parks anyway? What does the award element add?

Our discussions have shown that support for the scheme is very mixed, with some strong advocates and others that are critical of the scheme. It can be difficult to encourage car park operators to improve security in the face of other financial imperatives and it has been suggested that the award scheme is one of the few levers at the disposal of the police to encourage security improvements to be made. We would conclude that the award scheme has helped to reduce both crime and fear of crime and has acted as the driver for car park improvements in some areas but note that the SCP scheme is not the only way to improve the security of car parks[43] (and car park security has improved in some locations where the scheme has not been adopted).

---

43. Some of these alternative approaches have not, however, been fully researched and evaluated.

In summary:

- SCP can help reduce levels of vehicle crime and fear of crime *when targeted at high- crime car parks;*

- formal surveillance (including patrols), lighting, access control and a good physical appearance of the car park can lead to reductions in levels of crime and fear of crime in car parks;

- car park management appears to be a critical factor in running a safe, secure car park;

- new car parks built to SCP standard generally have low crime levels and are highly rated by users;

- car parks with lowest user ratings were all old surface car parks;

  - ❑ crime levels in these car parks were generally higher than in better ranked surface car parks;

  - ❑ they tend to be lacking in formal surveillance and have poorly defined perimeters;

- improving the security of car parks can lead to increased usage and profits;

- there is some evidence that there is some inconsistent application of the scheme across the country. However, whilst security standards vary, awards tend to be given to car parks that delivered low crime levels;

- take-up of the scheme has been slow in some areas and public awareness of the scheme is relatively low; and

- the importance of the award scheme in reducing crime is likely to increase if both the number of award scheme car parks and public awareness of the scheme increases. It has been suggested that increased public awareness may assist the scheme to overcome the main stumbling blocks to its expansion of poor industry response to the scheme in the light of costs of upgrading to SCP standards and little or no pressure for improvements in the market place.

The way forward

As we noted in Chapter 1, SCP scheme, the management of the award scheme has recently altered. A number of alterations to the scheme are planned as a result of this change. For example, there are plans to increase the number of RDMs and to amend the guidance manual and steps are being taken to move from an annual inspection regime to biennial inspections. An SCP web site (www.securedcarparks.co.uk) and marketing strategy are also being developed. These changes are likely to address some of the issues raised during this evaluation, such as the low public awareness of the scheme and concerns over the cost of annual inspections. It is, however, too early for the effect of these changes to be assessed. A number of recommendations emerge from our evaluation:

- The evaluators were made aware of problems relating to the overall format and administration of the scheme, which would warrant a thorough examination of the scheme's organisation and structure. One of the main outcomes of the review should be the development of a strategic plan, describing how the scheme will be taken forward. The lack of such a plan, in our view, has been one of the causes behind the slow development of the scheme. The review should also consider how the scheme links to the DfT[44], which has responsibility for both transport and planning issues (both of which have a large impact on car parks) and for Best Value (under which the performance of local authority parking services departments are reviewed). The review should also consider the naming of the scheme, which has caused concern for many car park operators, as well as possible methods of increasing the incentive for operators to join the scheme;

- this review of the scheme should include a consideration of ways in which inconsistencies in the application of the scheme can be eradicated[45]. Improved training for RDMs and ALOs was a commonly suggested solution to the problem of inconsistency. The majority of people attending the workshops indicated that they had not received any formal training on conducting assessments of car parks for the award scheme. This was confirmed by the survey, which showed that two-thirds of respondents (44) had not received any training. Those that had recently taken up their post were most likely to say that they had received training. Other structural and procedural methods of improving consistency should also be considered;

---

44. The DfT already runs the Secure Station scheme: a similar scheme to SCP aimed at improving safety at railway stations.
45. We would distinguish between flexibility and inconsistency. The scheme rightly involves elements of flexibility (as, for example, requirements may differ between car parks in different locations) but this needs to be exercised appropriately if it is not to lead to the kind of inconsistency that we found in some cases.

- if the scheme is primarily seen as a crime prevention tool, then greater emphasis should be placed on targeting high-crime car parks. Methods for encouraging higher crime car parks to improve security, such as targeted funding, should be considered;

- some car park operators, and others, have suggested that the SCP award should be expanded and become a general car parking standards award (along the lines of hotel 'star ratings', etc.). For example, the award could cover other aspects of car parks such as quality of car park surfacing, bay markings, ease of parking, etc. This should be given greater consideration, especially because of the importance that the general appearance of car parks appears to have on fear of crime levels;

- improvements should be made to the administrator's database that records details of scheme members. We note that action is being taken by the new scheme administrators to update and upgrade the database;

- improvements need to be made to the collection of both crime and disorder data for car parks to allow a problem-solving approach to be adopted. Ways of improving police systems for recording crime and disorder in car parks and reporting information to car park operators should be investigated;

- car parks operators are required under the award to keep a record of crime and other incidents in their car parks to allow them to adopt a problem-solving approach to crime prevention. Our study showed that this was not always being insisted upon by surveyors and that it was not being routinely used where information was being collected (often because of the format in which information was being collected). The NCP provides an example of a good system for recording incident data in their car parks (Box 5.2). It should be recognised that all crimes may not be reported to car park operators and some may only be reported directly to the police (this is most likely to be true in car parks which are not staffed, for example pay-and-display car parks). A two-way flow of information between the police and car parks operators is, therefore, required.

Box 5.2: The NCP's BROMAT system

The NCP record details of incidents in their car parks on their BROMAT system. BROMAT is an acronym for Break-ins to vehicles, Robberies against NCP, Offences against customers, Miscellaneous, Assaults on staff, Theft of vehicles. Information is computerised and can be interrogated by members of NCP's Security Department.

The NCP accept that their data will be incomplete. In particular, they suggest that crimes in pay-and-display car parks, where there are no facilities for reporting crime, are likely to be under-represented in their figures. One police officer has suggested that the BROMAT figures are likely to exclude some major crimes, which are more likely to be reported directly to the police, but to include more minor offences that would otherwise go unreported. The BROMAT figures do, however, allow the company to monitor trends in crime problems and to undertake some basic crime pattern analysis. Where possible, the company compares its figures to local crime figures to see if both sets of figures are revealing similar patterns.

- consideration should be given to making it a requirement for Crime and Disorder Reduction Partnerships to publish statistics of crime in local car parks[46]. Alternatively, this could be done by the local authority or police authority under the Best Value regime. This would allow car park users to make informed decisions about where they park their car and also act as an incentive for owners of higher crime car parks to make security improvements. We have seen one example of where the threat of 'naming and shaming' has encouraged one car park to take steps to address a crime problem (Box 2.1). Some interviewees suggested that if a decision was taken locally to adopt a 'naming and shaming' approach then this could sour local relationships. This problem is, however, removed if to do so is made a national requirement. Such an approach may also provide the impetus needed to encourage police forces to improve their recording of crime in car parks; and

- it is generally recognised that public awareness of the scheme needs to be increased and that this will possibly stimulate demand for the scheme. The JSG and BPA are currently developing a marketing strategy to achieve this. Awareness is also likely to increase following the launch of the forthcoming SCP website. Increased public awareness needs to go hand-in-hand with an increase in membership of the scheme (a 'chicken-and-egg' situation). The scheme's administrators suggest that the scheme needs a critical mass of around 3,000 members.

---

46.   We are aware of at least one area where car park crime statistics are published regularly in the local newspaper.

Appendix 1:   Cost-effectiveness tables

Table A.1: St John's surface car park

Car park capacity	160	vehicle spaces
Number of users (vehicles)	138,000	per annum
Additional income to the operator attributable to the achievement of SCP standards	£33,338	per annum
Average additional cost to the operator attributable to the achievement of SCP standards, including annual re-inspection	£500	per annum
Decline in the number of incidents of theft of vehicles consequent on SCP standards	9	per annum
Reduction in the costs to the owners of vehicles due to theft of vehicles consequent on SCP standards	£36,000	per annum [= 9 x £4,000][47]
Reduction in costs in the criminal justice system attributable to decline in thefts of vehicles	£693	per annum [= 9 x £77][36]
Decline in the number of incidents of theft from a vehicle consequent on SCP standards	0	per annum
Reduction in the costs to the owners of vehicles due to theft from vehicles consequent on SCP standards	0	per annum
Reduction in costs in the criminal justice system attributable to decline in thefts from vehicles	0	per annum
Decline in the number of incidents of criminal damage/vehicle interference consequent on SCP standards	4	per annum
Decline in cost to owners of vehicles of criminal damage/vehicle interference	£1,000	per annum [= 4 x £250][36]
Reduction in costs to the criminal justice system due to the reduction in criminal damage/vehicle interference	£40	per annum [= 4 x £10][36]

Hence

1. Benefit to users

Reduction in total costs to owners of vehicles due to reduction in crime attributable to SCP standards	£37,000	per annum
This is equivalent to a reduction in costs to vehicle owners of	**£0.27**	**per user**

47.   See Home Office Guidance document "The economic and social costs of crime" Sam Brand and Richard Price; Home Office, Research Development and Statistics (2000).

And

2. Benefits to the criminal justice system

Reduction in total costs to the criminal justice system due to reduction in crime – attributable to SCP standards	*£733*	*per annum*
This is equivalent to a reduction in costs to the criminal justice system of	*£0.005*	*per user*

Which may be compared with

3. Costs borne by the operator

The total improvement in operating cost (including additional revenue, attributable to the achievement of SCP standards)	£32,838	per annum
"One-off" capital costs of the scheme	£500	
Capital costs amortised over 10 years and assuming interest at 6% [=Cost*0.1359]		
Total of operating and amortised capital costs, improvement	*£32,770*	*Per annum*
This is equivalent to a total improvement of operating and amortised capital costs, per parking space, of:	*£205*	*per annum*
Or	*£0.24*	*per user*

Table A.2: The Ridings surface car park

Car park capacity	60	vehicle spaces
Number of users (vehicles)	88,000	per annum
Additional income to the operator attributable to the achievement of SCP standards	£40,000	per annum
Average additional cost to the operator attributable to the achievement of SCP standards, including re-inspection and lower clean-up costs	£2,000	per annum
Decline in the number of incidents of theft of vehicles consequent on SCP standards	2	per annum
Reduction in the costs to the owners of vehicles due to theft of vehicles consequent on SCP standards	£8,000	per annum [= 2 x £4,000][48]
Reduction in costs in the criminal justice system attributable to decline in thefts of vehicles	£154	per annum [= 2 x £77][37]
Decline in the number of incidents of theft from a vehicle consequent on SCP standards	22	Per annum

48.   see Home Office Guidance document "The economic and social costs of crime" Sam Brand and Richard Price; Home Office, Research Development and Statistics (2000)

Reduction in the costs to the owners of vehicles due to theft from vehicles consequent on SCP standards	£10,560	per annum [=22x£480]
Reduction in costs in the criminal justice system attributable to decline in thefts from vehicles	£660	per annum [=22x£30]
Decline in the number of incidents of criminal damage/vehicle interference consequent on SCP standards	5	Per annum
Decline in cost to owners of vehicles of criminal damage/vehicle interference	£1,250	Per annum [=5 x £250][37]
Reduction in costs to the criminal justice system due to the reduction in criminal damage/vehicle interference	£50	Per annum [=5 x £10][37]

Hence

1. Benefit to users

Reduction in total costs to owners of vehicles due reduction in crime attributable to SCP standards	£19,810	Per annum
This is equivalent to a reduction in costs to vehicle owners of	*£0.23*	*per user*

And

2. Benefits to the criminal justice system

Reduction in total costs to the criminal justice system due to reduction in crime attributable to SCP standards	*£864*	*Per annum*
This is equivalent to reduction in costs to the criminal justice system of	*£0.010*	*Per user*

Which may be compared with

3. Costs borne by the operator

The total improvement in operating costs [including additional income from charges, reduction in the cost of vandalism etc. and additional running costs]	£42,000	Per annum
"one-off" capital costs of the scheme	£20,300	
*Capital costs amortised over 10 years and assuming interest at 6% [=Cost*0.1359]*		
Total of operating and amortised capital costs, improvement	*£39,241*	*per annum*
This is equivalent to a total improvement of operating and amortised capital costs, per parking space, of:	*£654*	*per annum*
Or	*£0.45*	*per user*

Table A.3: New White Centre multi-storey car park

Car park capacity	1,100	vehicle spaces
Number of users (vehicles)	550,000	per annum
Annual additional income attributed to the achievement of SCP standards	£125,000	per annum
Average additional cost to the operator attributable to the achievement of SCP standards, including annual re-inspection	£100,000	per annum
Decline in the number of incidents of theft of vehicles consequent on SCP standards	6	per annum
Reduction in the costs to the owners of vehicles due to theft of vehicles consequent on SCP standards	£24,000	per annum [= 6 x £4,000][49]
Reduction in costs in the criminal justice system attributable to decline in thefts of vehicles	£462	per annum [= 6 x £77][38]
Decline in the number of incidents of theft from a vehicle consequent on SCP standards	53	per annum
Reduction in the costs to the owners of vehicles due to theft from vehicles consequent on SCP standards	£25,440	per annum [=53x£480]
Reduction in costs in the criminal justice system attributable to decline in thefts from vehicles	£1,590	per annum [=53x£30]
Decline in the number of incidents of criminal damage/vehicle interference consequent on SCP standards	10	per annum
Decline in cost to owners of vehicles of criminal damage/vehicle interference	£2,500	per annum [= 10 x £250][38]
Reduction in costs to the criminal justice system due to the reduction in criminal damage/vehicle interference	£100	per annum [= 10 x £10][38]
Hence		
1. Benefit to users		
Reduction in total costs to owners of vehicles due to reduction in crime attributable to SCP standards	£51,940	per annum
This is equivalent to a reduction in costs to vehicle owners of	£0.09	*per user*
And		

---

49.   see Home Office Guidance document "The economic and social costs of crime" Sam Brand and Richard Price; Home Office, Research Development and Statistics (2000).

2. Benefits to the criminal justice system

Reduction in total costs to the criminal justice system due to reduction in crime – attributable to SCP standards	*£2,152*	*per annum*
This is equivalent to a reduction in costs to the criminal justice system of	*£0.004*	*per user*

Benefits to users and to the criminal justice system may be compared with

3. Costs borne by the operator

The total improvement in operating cost (including additional revenue, attributable to the achievement of SCP standards, less additional operating costs)	£25,000	per annum
"one-off" capital costs of the scheme	£200,000	
Capital costs amortised over 10 years and assuming interest at 6% [=Cost*0.1359]		
Total of operating and amortised capital costs, increase	*£2,180*	*per annum*
This is equivalent to a total increase in operating and amortised capital costs, per parking space, of:	*£2*	*per annum*
Or	*£0.004*	*per user*

Table A.4: Main Victoria Centre multi-storey car park

Car park capacity	1,700	vehicle spaces
Number of users (vehicles)	600,000	vehicles per annum
Annual additional income attributed to the achievement of SCP standards	£150,000	per annum
Average additional cost to the operator attributable to the achievement of SCP standards, including annual re-inspection	£130,000	per annum
Decline in the number of incidents of theft of vehicles consequent on SCP status	6	per annum
Reduction in the costs to the owners of vehicles due to theft of vehicles consequent on SCP status	£24,000	per annum [= 6 x £4,000][50]
Reduction in costs in the criminal justice system attributable to decline in thefts of vehicles	£462	per annum [= 6 x £77][39]
Decline in the number of incidents of theft from a vehicle consequent on SCP status	32	per annum

50. see Home Office Guidance document "The economic and social costs of crime" Sam Brand and Richard Price; Home Office, Research Development and Statistics (2000).

Reduction in the costs to the owners of vehicles due to theft from vehicles consequent on SCP status	£15,360	per annum [=32x£480]
Reduction in costs in the criminal justice system attributable to decline in thefts from vehicles	£960	per annum [=32x£30]
Decline in the number of incidents of criminal damage/vehicle interference consequent on SCP status	6	per annum
Decline in cost to owners of vehicles of criminal damage/vehicle interference	£1,500	per annum [= 6 x £250][39]
Reduction in costs to the criminal justice system due to the reduction in criminal damage/vehicle interference	£60	per annum [= 6 x £10][1]

Hence

1. Benefit to users

Reduction in total costs to owners of vehicles due to reduction in crime attributable to SCP standards	£40,860	per annum
This is equivalent to a reduction in costs to vehicle owners of £0.07	*per user*	

And

2. Benefits to the criminal justice system

Reduction in total costs to the criminal justice system due to reduction in crime – attributable to SCP standards	*£1,482*	*per annum*
Reduction in costs to the criminal justice system, per car park user	*£0.002*	*per user*

Benefits to users and to the criminal justice system may be compared with

Costs borne by the operator

The total improvement in operating cost (including additional revenue, attributable to the achievement of SCP standards, less additional operating costs)	£20,000	per annum
"one-off" capital costs of the scheme	£200,000	
Capital costs amortised over 10 years and assuming interest at 6% [=Cost*0.1359]		
Total of operating and amortised capital costs, increase	*£7,180*	*per annum*
This is equivalent to a total increase in operating and amortised capital costs, per parking space, of:	*£4.22*	*per annum*
or	*£0.012*	*Per user*

References

10 Downing Street website (2002) Boosts for fight against car crime. 11 February 2002. (www.pm.gov.uk/PrintMe.asp?pageid=6066&date=11+February+2002).

AA (2002) Demanding Safer Parking. theAAmagazine. London: John Brown Publishing Ltd.

Abbott, J. and Fried, G. (1999) Asphalt Jungle: Providing Parking-Area Security through Design and Common Sense, Cornell Hotel and Restaurant Administration Quarterly, Vol 40, No 2, p 46-53.

Barclay, G., Tavares, C. and Siddique, A. (2001) International comparisons of criminal justice statistics. Home Office Statistics Bulletin Issue 6/01. London: Home Office.

Barclay, P. *et al.* (1997) Preventing Auto Theft in Commuter Lots: a bike patrol in Vancouver, in Clarke R.V. (editor), Situational Crime Prevention: successful case studies. 2nd Edition. New York: Harrow and Heston p 143-156.

Brand, S. and Price, R. (2000) The Economic and Social Costs of Crime. Home Office Research Study 217. Home Office: London.

Brown, B. (1995) CCTV in Town Centres: Three Case Studies. Police Research Group Crime Detection and Prevention Series Paper 68. London: Home Office.

Building (1968) Rochester Row Car Park: the latest development in Westminster's parking policy. Building 8 November 1968.

CERF (2001) Evaluation of the Trevipark Automated Parking System (Draft). Civil Engineering Research Foundation: Washington (http://www.cerf.org/ceitec/eval/ongoing/draft.pdf).

Connaught (1998) The Connaught Car Park Report: Helping to make multi-storey car parks the first option for motorists. Connaught Specialist Contracts Ltd: Bristol.

Davey, C., Cooper, R. and Press, M. (2001) Case Study Exemplars, Produced by the Design Policy Partnership for the Design Against Crime programme, supported by the Design Council, Home Office and DTI (www.designagainstcrime.org).

Eck, J. and Spelman, W. (1992) Thefts from Vehicles in Shipyard Parking Lots, in Clarke R.V. (editor), Situational Crime Prevention: successful case studies. 2nd Edition. New York: Harrow and Heston p 164-173.

ETRA (1998) Environment, Transport and Regional Affairs – Tenth Report (www.publications.parliament.uk/pa/cm199798/cmselect/cmenvtra/495/49502.htm)

Hardy, E. (1998) Vehicle Theft in Europe The Unofficial Redistribution of Vehicles. Public Policy Research Centre, International Car Distribution Programme Ltd, Research Report 3/98 (unpublished).

Kershaw, C. et al. (2001) The 2001 British Crime Survey. Home Office Statistical Bulletin. Home Office: London

Laycock, G.K. (1992) Operation Identification, or the Power of Publicity?, in Clarke R.V. (editor), Situational Crime Prevention: successful case studies. 2nd Edition. New York: Harrow and Heston p 230-238.

Laycock, G. and Austin, C. (1992) Crime prevention in parking facilities. Security Journal, vol 3, p 154-160.

Light, R., Nee, C. and Ingham, H. (1993) Car theft: the offender's perspective. Home Office Research Study No 130. London: Home Office.

Lydall, R. (2002) Parking fees and fines cost drivers £340 million a year. Evening Standard. Friday August 9 2002.

Mayhew, P. and van Dijk, J.J.M. (1997) Criminal Victimisation in Eleven Industrialised Countries Key Findings from the 1996 International Crime Victims Survey. Onderzoek en Beleid, vol 167. Netherlands: WODC.

McDonagh, E., Wortley, R. and Homel, R. (2002) Perceptions of physical, psychological, social and legal deterrents to joyriding. Crime and Community Safety: An International Journal, vol 4, p 11-25.

Moss, K. and Pease, K. (1999) Crime and Disorder Act 1998: Section 17 A Wolf in Sheep's Clothing? Crime and Community Safety: An International Journal, vol 1, p 15-19.

Moss, K. and Seddon, M. (2001) Crime Prevention and Planning: Searching for Common Sense in Disorder Legislation. Crime and Prevention and Community Safety: An International Journal, vol 3, p 25-31.

Moster, H. and Longmore-Etheridge, A. (2000) A Good Parking Space. Security Management. p 62-68.

Nelson, A. (1997) Fear of Parking. Town and County Planning, vol 66, p 3.

Painter, K. A. and Farrington, D. P. (1997) The Crime Reducing Effect of Improved Street Lighting: The Dudley Project in Clarke R.V. (editor), Situational Crime Prevention: successful case studies. 2nd Edition. New York: Harrow and Heston p 209-226.

Painter, K. A. and Farrington, D. P. (2001) Evaluating Situational Crime Prevention Using a Young People's Survey. British Journal of Criminology, vol 41, p 266-284.

Parking Review (2001) Management Survey 2001, Issue 122, p 18-24.

Parking Review (2002a) British Parking Awards 2002, Issue 125, p 18.

Parking Review (2002b) Edinburgh Autosafe Solves Urban Squeeze, Issue 123, p 27-29.

Parking Today (2000) It works, License Plate Recognition at Phoenix Sky Harbor. Parking Today, vol 5, issue 2 (http://docs.vircomnet.com/mobility/parking_vc/phoenix.htm).

Pengelly, R. (2000) Designing Out Crime. Police Magazine. Police Federation.

Povey, D. and Colleagues (2001) Recorded Crime England and Wales, 12 Months to March 2001. London: Home Office

Poyner, B. (1997) Situational Crime Prevention in Two Parking Facilities, in Clarke R.V. (editor), Situational Crime Prevention: successful case studies. 2nd Edition. New York: Harrow and Heston p 157-166.

RAC (1991) Cars in cities: how to tackle congestion and improve the quality of life. Policy Leaflet 5. London: RAC (quoted in Webb et al., 1992).

Sallybanks, J. and Brown, R. (1999) Vehicle Crime Reduction: Turning the Corner, Police Research Unit Series Paper 119, London: Home Office.

Schneider, R.H. and Kitchen, T. (2002) Planning for Crime Prevention: A TransAtlantic Perspective. London: Routledge.

Slobodian, P.J. and Browne, K.D. (2001) A Review of Car Crime in England and Wales. British Journal of Social Work, vol. 31, p 465-480.

Smith, M.S. (1996) Crime Prevention through Environmental Design in Parking Facilities. Research in Brief. Washington DC: National Institute of Justice.

Smith, M.S. (1996) Crime Prevention through Environmental Design in Parking Facilities. Research in Brief. Washington DC: National Institute of Justice.

Smyth, B. (1993) Brightening Up Car parks. Crime Prevention News. London: Home Office.

Tilley, N. (1993) Understanding Car Parks, Crime and CCTV: Evaluation Lessons from Safer Cities. Police Research Group, Crime Prenvetion Unit Paper 42. London: Home Office.

URBED (1994) Vital and Viable Town Centres: Meeting the Challenge. London: HMSO.

WCJ (1999a) Secure Car Park Scheme Teleresearch (unpublished report June 1999).

WCJ (1999b) Secure Car Park Scheme Teleresearch: Addendum to June 1999 Research (unpublished report October 1999).

Webb, B., Brown, B., and Bennett, K. (1992) Preventing Crime in Car Parks. Crime Prevention Unit Series Paper 34, London: Home Office.

Webster, D. and Pengelley, R. (1997) ParkSafe 97 The Secured Car Parks Scheme. Thame: The Thames Valley Partnership.

Welsh, B.C. and Farrington, D.P. (2002) Crime Prevention Effects of Closed Circuit Television: A Systematic Review. London: Home Office.

Which? 1990 Pay and Dismay. p 330-333.

Wilson, J.Q. and Kelling, G.L. (1982) Broken Windows. The Atlantic Monthly, p 29-38.

Wraige, H. (2001) Parking's Lot, Professional Engineering, vol 14, p 43.

Notes

Notes

Notes

RDS Publications

Requests for Publications

Copies of our publications and a list of those currently available may be obtained from:

Home Office
Research, Development and Statistics Directorate
Communication Development Unit
Room 275, Home Office
50 Queen Anne's Gate
London SW1H 9AT
Telephone: 020 7273 2084 (answerphone outside of office hours)
Facsimile: 020 7222 0211
E-mail: publications.rds@homeoffice.gsi.gov.uk

alternatively

why not visit the RDS website at
Internet: http://www.homeoffice.gov.uk/rds/index.html

where many of our publications are available to be read on screen or downloaded for printing.